OFF GRID SOLAR POWER

Step-By-Step Guide to Make Your Own Solar Power System For RV's, Boats, Tiny Houses, Cars, Cabins and More

Small Footprint Press

© **Copyright 2022 - All rights reserved.**

The content contained within this book may not be reproduced, duplicated or transmitted without direct written permission from the author or the publisher.

Under no circumstances will any blame or legal responsibility be held against the publisher, or author, for any damages, reparation, or monetary loss due to the information contained within this book, either directly or indirectly.

Legal Notice:

This book is copyright protected. It is only for personal use. You cannot amend, distribute, sell, use, quote or paraphrase any part, or the content within this book, without the consent of the author or publisher.

Disclaimer Notice:

Please note the information contained within this document is for educational and entertainment purposes only. All effort has been executed to present accurate, up to date, reliable, complete information. No warranties of any kind are declared or implied. Readers acknowledge that the author is not engaged in the rendering of legal, financial, medical or professional advice. The content within this book has been derived from various sources. Please consult a licensed professional before attempting any techniques outlined in this book.

By reading this document, the reader agrees that under no circumstances is the author responsible for any losses, direct or indirect, that are incurred as a result of the use of the information contained within this document, including, but not limited to, errors, omissions, or inaccuracies.

CONTENTS

Introduction 2

Chapter 1:
Solar Power Explained 12

Chapter 2:
Electricity 101 33

Chapter 3:
How To Choose The Right Battery 52

Chapter 4:
How To Choose The Right Solar Panel 66

Chapter 5:
How To Choose The Right Wires, Fuses, And Inverter 83

Chapter 6:
Build Your Own Solar Power System 103

Chapter 7:
Blueprints And Equations 126

Conclusion 144

References 153

INTRODUCTION

I'd put my money on the sun and solar energy. What a source of power!

—Thomas Edison

Solar power has evolved to become an environmentally friendly, renewable source of energy and an affordable and cost-saving source of power. Its applications are endless, and improvements in the cost and efficiency of solar systems have skyrocketed over the past decade to the point where it is cheaper globally to produce power using solar arrays than using coal.

Our sun truly is the source of all life and energy on the planet, and we would be doing such a disservice to the environment if we didn't get more energy directly from this source. Solar power is reliable and predictable. You can easily track it based on the sun's intensity to the point where clouds passing and blocking out the sun will cause a noticeable drop in the energy produced by solar panels.

Solar systems are relatively straightforward to design and install. Of course, this is compared to other sources of energy, such as hydroelectric, natural gas, diesel, coal, wind, and geothermal energy. Most of these are far more complex, require far more capital and resources, and are not renewable. A common misunderstanding is that making use of a backup diesel generator is cheaper than using solar. This is only the case for people who think of the capital cost of buying the equipment. The actual cost of ownership for anything is in both the capital and operational costs. When considering this, you can see that, over the space of, say, five to ten years, using a diesel generator is more costly. You have to refuel it, replace filters and oil, and provide any other services required to keep it operational. You are also stuck with the noise that they make as well as the fumes that go everywhere. Hardly what you want for an off-grid solution. Compare this to a solar system which, once installed, essentially only needs to be cleaned. That's about it when it comes to regular maintenance. Every once in a while, you may have a damaged fuse, or you may be unfortunate enough to have lightning strike your panels, but these occasions are very few and far between.

Solar systems also have the benefit of battery backup systems. This takes out the argument that you can only have power when the sun is shining, far from it. When the sun is shining, you can make use of the energy and charge your batteries simultaneously, then make use of the energy stored at night just as though you were making use of the utility electricity supply. It really starts to look attractive when you look closer at your return of investment (ROI) on a solar system. This is essentially the time it takes for the solar system to save you the money equivalent to what you paid for the system in the first place. It is not uncommon for these systems to have an ROI period of around seven years. For a system that you could have in place for 25 years, paying it off over seven years and then actively saving money for the next 18 years is mind-boggling.

This is especially true for residential solar systems. When you start to look closely at your monthly electricity bill and see the figures drop due to your newly installed solar system, you will wonder why you didn't install your own solar system years ago!

We are Small Print Press, and we are committed to helping you sustainably survive and thrive while ensuring together that the world is a better place for future generations to come. Our mission is to empower people to mitigate all risks of potential disasters for themselves and their loved ones while still enjoying life and without living in fear. Having an off-grid solar power system in place is essential when dealing with natural disasters or becoming more self-sufficient.

Furthermore, it is only logical to make use of renewable energy moving forward. When it comes to things such as fossil fuels, coal, and natural gasses, we are limited by the quantity of these products that exist on the earth. You can compare it to engaging in a hunter and gatherer lifestyle versus a subsistence farming lifestyle. As much as you move from place to place, hunting contributes to the desolation of food resources in each region you travel through. These resources will never be able to supplement their reserves based on how quickly we consume them. Ancient populations started ballooning, and the hunter and gatherer lifestyle stopped making sense. Raising animals and crops in a set location made more sense for feeding the population. Over time, people could continue to grow more crops and raise more domesticated animals to feed expanding populations. Relying on a dwindling wild animal population made less and less sense. Renewable energy makes sense because we are reducing our reliance on finite resources that are dwindling just as wild game would dwindle with an expanding hunter population.

We at Small Footprint Press are fully aware of the detrimental impact we are having on the environment. We are consuming resources that have an expiration date without a concrete plan to address this problem. Moreover, we are burning fossil fuels to support our lifestyles and expanding global population while having unequivocal evidence that this behavior affects our climate and results in weather conditions that have significant consequences for our longevity on this planet. We want to create a lifestyle that is not destructive to our own lives and the ecosystems on this planet. It's often easy to forget that the tens of thousands of other species that live in this world have been here since long before we came around. These diverse animals, plants, fungi, birds, reptiles, bacteria, and everything in between all live on earth with us. We are still animals, just the same as they are. The only thing separating us is our intellect and recognition of others as individuals with their own conscience and thinking capability. We cannot continue on the path we are walking down because it will push us into a mass extinction event, which some already proclaim that we are in. This will escalate until all living things as we know them will die or change, and, most importantly, we will die off as well. However, the world will continue on. Life will continue on. We need to look past our greed to ensure our survival and longevity on earth.

It's not all gloom and doom, as we have been given the opportunity to make a change in our lifestyle. Although it may seem like a drop in the ocean to change your personal energy usage, if millions of people share the same mentality, then the power is with us. We are one with this world and need it to thrive for us to thrive. Our impact on the environment is unquestionable when looking at all evidence provided by science. We need to be more responsible and conscious. If we change by accelerating the transition to sustainable living and generating our own renewable energy for consumption, we are taking a step in the right direction.

Don't be disheartened by people telling you that the raw materials for solar systems require fossil fuels and that it negates its impact on the global climate, as these claims have been clearly debunked. It has been conclusively proven that solar panels themselves, made up of silicon, glass, copper, and aluminum, require at most two years of operation to generate as much power as was required to produce them (Svarc, 2019). The same can be said for lithium-ion batteries, which is a hot topic of discussion. Arguments arise from the mining of lithium, which is less labor and energy-intensive than the mining of aluminum. For the most part, lithium is a byproduct of other processes, such as brines, which account for half of all lithium produced from manufacturers. This means that the energy required to produce lithium-ion batteries could be provided using power generated by lithium-ion batteries, and it would still be productive energy. Essentially, it is an energy positive product, meaning that more energy can be generated from its extraction from the earth than would be consumed by extracting it (Talens Peiró et al., 2013). If you are ever confronted by people who argue that your solar system is more harmful to the environment than it benefits it, be sure to offer them these scientifically proven facts.

This book will go over all of the concepts around solar systems and how you can install your own. It will cover the basic overview of what solar power is, how you can design an effective solar system, and help you choose from all the different products out there in the market. You will be taken through some concepts around electricity so that, even if you have no knowledge in this field, you will be capable of installing your own solar system. We want to highlight now, and will do so again consistently in this book, the importance of safety whenever working with electricity. It is still very dangerous at the end of the day, so you must take the correct precautions, wear personal protective equipment (PPE), and follow the best practices. PPE consists of clothing designed to protect you. When installing and testing your solar system, insulated gloves and safety boots are the most important items to protect yourself from injury.

It is also important to inform you that there are laws and standards around using solar systems, particularly when you are interconnected with your electricity supplier. This book will cover some of the basics, but they vary from state to state and country to country. They are in place for a reason, and it isn't difficult to ensure that you comply with them and work with them to make sure that you have the best system possible.

If, on the other hand, you are installing a completely off-grid solution, then you only need to follow standards and safety precautions for your own benefit and don't necessarily need to register with your electricity supplier. It is a positive thing to see various laws and standards being processed by electricity suppliers because it shows that they support consumers making use of solar as much as possible. This book will focus on the small-scale, off-grid solar systems that you can install yourself. The primary focus areas will be in Recreational Vehicles (RV's), cabins, tiny homes, cars, boats, and other residential areas, such as larger homes. There are many similarities in how the systems work. The main difference is in the physical scale, installation procedures, and specific products necessary for particular applications, such as water-tight units for boat applications.

In the twenty-first century, there is a renewed drive for people to become more self-reliant and sustainable. You can reduce your carbon footprint, help the environment, save money, reduce your risk of calamities and generate your own clean energy to use however you choose. The only thing it requires is time, energy, and initial capital cost. Other than that, there is absolutely nothing to lose in installing your very own solar system. By the end of this book, you will be fully equipped to do it yourself!

Chapter 1:
Solar Power Explained

In this chapter, we will cover the concepts behind solar power and how it is possible to capture solar energy. We will discuss the terminology that you can expect to come across and the various components that make up a solar-powered installation. Don't get disheartened if it seems like a lot to take in. Over time, you will realize that solar systems are straightforward and not overly complex. This makes it the perfect DIY project to pursue.

This chapter should give you a good background on how to go about designing, installing, and testing a solar system, as well as the basics of what it entails. It isn't an overload of information and lets you know what you are getting into when installing your own solar system. In the following chapters, we will expand more on concepts, theories, and how the various components work and are integrated with one another.

What is Solar Power and How Does it Work?

Lying at the center of our solar system is a gigantic, burning fusion reactor: the sun. Every second of every day, hydrogen is converted into helium on a massive scale, releasing heat, light, and energy. The light the sun releases arrives on earth in the form of photons. Each photon carries energy, and solar power is our way of harnessing that energy (Marsh, 2019). Solar power is harvested from what is known as solar irradiance. This essentially means that the more intense the sunlight is, the more energy it carries with it. This means that you can harness more energy per solar panel in light-intense areas.

It is interesting to note that humans are not the first species to harness the energy from the sun. Most plants use photosynthesis to convert carbon dioxide and water into carbohydrates with energy from the sun. It is a process necessary for life as we know it on the planet. The earliest form of humans using energy from the sun was to light fires using a magnifying method well over one and a half millennia ago. This has changed a great deal over the years, and solar energy now makes up an estimated 2% of the world's total energy usage

(Ritchie & Roser, 2020). There are countless opportunities to elevate this quantity over the next decade as the world moves toward using more green energy and less energy generated from fossil fuels. The efficiency of converting energy from the sun into useful energy is not very high based on today's technology. This is not a cause of major concern, as even plants have a very low efficiency of using sunlight in the process of photosynthesis. As technology improves, our ability to absorb more energy will inevitably improve. The sun has been providing us with energy for billions of years. As humans, improving our ability to harness the sun is a testament to our initiative to seek out energy resources that will not run out or do major harm to our environment or communities living here.

The natural phenomena on earth are the main driving force behind generating more sustainable forms of electricity. We do need to consider the effects of drawing energy from natural forces such as hydroelectric power, as this may result in water channels being cut off when building dam walls. But, in cases such as wind power, tidal power from wave action in coastal areas, solar power, and geothermal energy, we are not impacting the environment in any measurable way. The wind will continue to blow in its course and have the same impact on the biosphere as we know it. Tides will continue to flow, and waves will continue to crash in coastal areas whether we harness this power or not. Geothermal heat will continue to be generated due to tectonic motion and pressure built up in the earth's crust, making use of this heat not harming the environment. The same goes for solar energy, which will strike the earth the same way it always has. The primary area of concern with any of these technologies is the energy required to get the raw materials necessary for the products that harness this energy.

Although there are areas of concern, such as inhumane working conditions for mine workers in many developing countries globally, most companies providing the raw materials have a strict ethical policy that seeks to improve and uplift communities surrounding mining areas. There are bad apples and those who will take advantage of communities or individuals, which is why transparency in major mining companies is required. We should never stop pressing these corporations to ensure that they can source raw materials such as copper, lithium, aluminum, and other raw materials ethically. These activities not doing more damage to the environment is just as important as the benefit gained in using them. If it uses more energy to extract lithium from the earth, then why would we use it in batteries as an energy storage method? It wouldn't make sense to burn more fossil fuels in extracting the products needed. All major manufacturers are aware of this, and it would make their product non-profitable, so scientific research is always ongoing to ensure that the direction we are moving in makes sense. There is no scientific evidence that extracting required raw materials outweighs the energy-saving capability of these products, so be sure not to alter your perception based on people who do not have any factual basis for their claims. The age of misinformation is upon us, and the only way to educate ourselves is to do our own research, look at the evidence and facts that are proven, and push to get answers in areas that we aren't certain about.

How Can You Harness Solar Power?

There are two ways in which we are able to generate electricity using energy from the sun. Thermal capturing is used far less for small-scale power generation and is only used in large-scale power generation plants. From the word thermal, you should recognize that this is a form of generating energy from the heat that is provided by the sun. There are also passive ways in which you can use this energy.

Solar thermal capturing is typically split into three categories: low, mid and high temperature. Low-temperature capturing is typically used in heating and cooling, mostly in buildings and living spaces. It is passive, and an example is letting natural light into your house for warmth in the winter and blocking the sun to keep a cool inside temperature during summer. The second form of solar thermal capturing is in mid temperatures. An example of this would be in using solar geysers. Heat is captured in collectors, and the heat energy is transferred to water in the geyser itself. It is a self-circulating system and a massive cost saver compared to geysers using electrical or gas elements. Finally, there are high-temperature solar thermal capturing systems. An example of this system would be concentrated solar plants that reflect sunlight using an array of reflector panels and focus it on tubes containing a fluid that absorbs thermal energy efficiently. The high amount of concentrated sunlight provides a large amount of heat absorbed by the fluid and used to turn water into steam and drive a turbine.

The other method of converting energy from the sun into electricity is using the photovoltaic process. The type of solar systems that we will focus on in this book are solar panels that make use of this process. All small-scale solar systems that generate electricity for homes, cabins, RV's, boats, and other vehicles use these solar panels. This is why many solar systems are referred to as photovoltaic (PV) arrays. It's helpful to understand this jargon and recognize why it is used. An array is a description of several panels mounted together to generate power.

How Do Solar Panels Convert Solar Energy into Usable Electricity?

There are two predominant ways in which energy from the sun can be harnessed to produce energy that is beneficial to us. The first of these methods, as I briefly discussed above, involves solar thermal energy capturing. Common procedures used to provide a function from this form of energy harvesting are solar geysers and solar concentrate plants. Solar geysers are mounted in order to absorb heat from the sun and used to circulate and heat water for usage, saving the electricity from using standard electrical and gas geysers, which require burning gas to heat water for cleaning, showering, and other practical purposes (Hutchison & Galiardi, 2019).

Another larger-scale example of making use of the thermal energy from the sun is concentrated in a solar plant. In these systems, hundreds of solar panels face a central tower, and this focused beam of light is used to superheat a solution that has been designed to retain heat very well.

A final form of this energy is in parabolic solar power plants. In these systems, solar panels are mounted in a c-shape, or parabola. These panels have a central line with water inside that is mounted at the focus point of the solar panels. The heat energy from the sun is focused on this central line, which typically carries water or another liquid that absorbs heat efficiently and can be superheated. The heat is then transferred to generate power. These systems are cheaper, as no cells are needed, only reflectors. They also have the advantage of not having a dependency on temperature and have a much longer lifespan than standard solar panels. However, they are far less energy efficient, still require cleaning, and take up a lot of physical space.

The other form of solar generation is the photovoltaic process. This is the process that typical solar systems use. When sunlight strikes the solar cells, typically made up of a semiconductive material such as silicon, it dislodges the semiconductor's electrons. These electrons are set in motion and flow to an area with a more positive charge. This is because electrons carry a negative charge and move to an area with a more positive charge via attraction. Likewise, the location where the electron starts becomes more negatively charged, this repels the electron away. In other words, a potential difference is set up between the electron's existing position and a more positive location, which results in the electrons moving and creating a flow of current. When the cells are connected in series, the potential difference across the cells increases while the flow of current through each cell remains the same. This boosts the power and is the reason why typical solar panels are the size that they are. They are small enough to be handled by a single person, easily replaceable, and robust enough in their manufacturing. They are also large enough to have each panel generate a significant amount of power. It would be more costly to build solar panels that are the size of a single cell, as more materials would be needed to build frames, increasing the cost of each unit significantly.

OFF-GRID VS. ON-GRID (AKA GRID-TIED) SOLAR ENERGY

There are two main types of solar arrays: off-grid and on-grid solar systems. To explain the difference between the two, we need to look at what is meant by "the grid." The electrical grid is the network of electrical infrastructure that connects all parts of a country, or even several countries, together. It includes generation, where energy is first produced; transmission, which is similar to the arteries transporting power to different parts of a country or country; and distribution, which takes electricity to every end-user. This electrical network is typically termed as the grid. There are standards, including quality and safety standards, that come with being tied into the grid. If you receive your power from a utility, then you are connected to the grid.

In terms of a solar system, if your solar system is connected to the grid in any way, then it is a grid-tied solution. A grid-tied solar system may or may not have a battery backup system, as you receive power from both your solar panels and the grid. This means that you don't necessarily require batteries. You need to register your solar system and have it approved by your electricity supplier. The main reason for this is that electricity suppliers need to know all the power sources on the grid. If you have a grid-tied solution, when the grid supply fails and you aren't supplied by them anymore, your system has to disconnect from the grid automatically. You can still supply power to yourself, but you cannot be connected to the grid. The reasoning behind this is simple enough. If power is turned off to a section of the grid where there is a fault, there can be nothing making that section live for safety reasons. If you haven't disconnected from the grid, you may make a grid section that needs to be worked on live. This would carry the risk of someone getting electrocuted and hurt because they are unaware of a power source. If the section is isolated, it should be safe to work on, and if it is isolated and the section is still found to be live, then figuring out where the power is coming from can waste time for those fixing the fault (August 12 & 2019, 2019).

The second option for a solar system is to have an off-grid system. In this system, the electrical network that you create is completely separate from the primary grid. You generate your own power and use it up while not connecting to the main electrical network. The advantage of this solution is that you can install your own backup battery system and be completely independent of the utility supply. In the long run, both systems will save you money. However, by using an off-grid system, the initial capital expense may be more than a grid-tied system, as you will probably need a larger solar system and would have to rewire several electrical connections. Still, in the long run, it will save you more money. This is partly because you will not be paying your monthly electricity usage, but also because you will not have to pay a maximum demand surcharge or a levy to have a connection to the utility.

THE FOUR MAIN COMPONENTS OF A SIMPLE OFF-GRID SOLAR POWER SYSTEM

A typical off-grid solar-powered system consists of four primary components: solar panels, battery chargers, batteries, and power inverters. Each of these four components plays a vital role and works together to provide you with electricity that you can use. Other smaller components come into play, and we will get into the details of these in Chapter 2.

The solar panels are the power source of a solar system. Each panel comprises dozens of photovoltaic cells that work together and generate direct current (DC) power. They are often termed modules, panels, or solar panels. They are connected either parallel or in a series to create what is described as a solar array. A solar array generates electricity at a suitable DC voltage and current for the inverter to convert to alternating current (AC). These are two different types of electricity, and some devices can convert electricity from one type to another. The description of these two different types of electricity, AC and DC, is included in Chapter 2 below.

The second component in a solar system is the battery chargers or charge controllers. When it comes to these units, there are several options to connect to the system. There are charge controllers that use the DC electricity generated by the solar panels and charge batteries directly from this power source. There are also battery chargers that can be connected after the inverter, which charge and manage your batteries. The final option is with certain brands of inverters that have a built-in battery charger. The purpose of the battery chargers is to enable power to flow to the batteries when they are charging and from the batteries when they are discharging. Batteries are able to store energy, but must be carefully charged with energy and discharged of stored energy. The battery chargers also need to protect the batteries from being damaged by short circuits or power surges. The main reason for this is that batteries are one of the most expensive solar system components.

The third component is the batteries themselves. There are a whole host of battery types that can be used, but their function remains the same. Batteries are designed to store energy by being charged when surplus power is generated by the solar panels, such as when the sun is shining. They are then used as the source of power when insufficient energy is supplied by the solar array, such as at night. Making use of batteries creates a stable and consistent power supply from your solar system. It is proposed to oversize your solar system, especially your battery backup because you cannot predict whether you will use more power than expected or if the weather will not be conducive to generating power consistently. If you have several days of cloudy weather, then your solar panels will not be able to generate as much power compared to when it is sunny. This means that the solar panels will not meet the energy demand that you have. If you have an undersized battery backup system, then you may get by for a few days, but once the batteries have been discharged, you will be left with no power at all!

The final component of your solar system is the inverter. Inverters are devices that convert electricity from DC to AC. AC is the form of electricity that is used in all typical households. Therefore, to use the type of power that devices make use of, you need to convert the type of power that solar panels generate. Inverters use semiconductors to convert electricity and typically have a filter that gives you good quality AC supply that is safe to connect all devices to. In the US, that supply is 110 volts (V) at a frequency of 60 hertz. In many other countries worldwide, the supply power is 230 V at a frequency of 50 hertz. The type of inverter you use depends on your region and what power is used.

These four main components work in unison to give you a fully functional solar system. The solar panels, or modules, generate power from sunlight, the batteries are charged with a battery charger, the batteries themselves store energy to be used when required, and the inverter converts the electricity to the standard electrical supply used in that region.

It is important to note that, beyond these four primary components that make up your solar system, there are also many more minor but still important things you will need to specify, design for, purchase, and install with your solar system. It is also of great importance that you thoroughly test your solar system to pick up on any defects or errors in how your system is set up and installed. Of course, it is far easier and cheaper to check for problems before you install your system at all, so making use of calculations and simulation software can greatly assist you in planning your system out. On average, you should go through three major phases in implementing your solar system, and each of these phases will take approximately the same amount of time.

Phases of Installation

The first phase is in designing your system. This includes determining where you want to install your solar system, how you want to go about the installation, and specifying the various components that you require. This includes sizing your solar panels as individual units and establishing the total number of panels that you will require. It also includes your batteries, inverter, battery charger or charge controller, tools, mounting equipment, wires, and safety practices that you should follow all the way through. You should carry out all your calculations and test your system using some form of software simulation. There are numerous software with free 30 day trials available to test if your system will work in the way you hope it will. This whole process can be called the planning phase.

The second part of your solar project is purchasing and adjudicating. You will have to research what solar panels, batteries, inverters, and charge controllers are available to you. There is no point in designing for an inverter that is readily available in Germany but extremely expensive with an extended delivery time to get to you in the US. There may also be several options that seem almost identical, and this is where you will need to adjudicate. It could be as simple as a pros and cons list to compare two different products in order to choose the best option for you. It could have a major impact on you if you go with a cheap option, only to discover later that many of the features you require do not come with the inverter or have to be purchased separately. During this phase, you should be able to narrow down your options and purchase them from suppliers. It is imperative that you get the installation manuals with these products to ensure that you follow the manufacturer's specifications on installing the products. This phase will often lead you to a point where you realize that something you had designed for in stage one is not practically feasible, and you will have to go back to tweak your design. There is nothing wrong with this, and you shouldn't feel disheartened if you go back more than once to adjust your design to match what is available to you on the market. It's an iterative process that you want to complete in this stage, preferably before you actually purchase the equipment.

The third and final stage is the installation and testing of your solar system. If you have managed to plan out your layout, equipment, and installation method, then things should go fairly smoothly. However, in practice, there are always things that you may have missed: a tool you may require, more wires, connectors, screws, or drill bits. Nothing will ever go entirely according to plan, but the better you have planned, the fewer headaches you will have during this stage. This is often termed teething problems in engineering because a new installation will give you more trouble than a system operating for a long time. You must prepare yourself for teething problems and remain attentive to them. Sometimes, it could be something minor, such as your solar panels being dirty or a fuse blowing when you first started testing your system. Other times, the problems are a bit more challenging to overcome, such as your solar panels not being installed correctly or a large tree casting a shadow over half of your solar panels.

In this final stage, you will also need to test and monitor how your system is operating. You can use clamp meters to measure current and multimeters to measure voltage to confirm that the power you are generating is in line with what you designed for. You will also need to test any safety devices, such as isolating your solar system safely for maintenance or replacements needed later on.

These three stages form the lifecycle of your solar project and, if you follow them, spend an equal amount of time on each phase, and don't skip any major steps, then your system will be successful. You will be fully geared up to generate your own electricity, save a lot of money in the long run, and always have a backup power source should the grid go down.

Chapter 2: Electricity 101

This chapter will go over general electricity concepts to make sense of solar systems and how to go about designing and installing them. By the end of this chapter, you should grasp the basic aspects of electricity that are relevant to solar systems.

Basic Forms of Power

To start, let us cover the two different types of electricity. These were mentioned in Chapter 1 and are known as AC and DC. AC has a voltage that alternates from positive to negative due to the charge of electrons when the power is generated, which is driven by the magnetic field. There are north and south poles of a magnet which result in the positive and negative charge. AC is named as such because the flow of electrons alternates between positive and negative. A sinusoidal wave flows along the path of electricity from the power source to where the power is used. Picture it as a wave that is generated when you throw a pebble into a pond. The waves flow away from where the pebble hits the water, and any single point experiences the water rising and falling as it moves past it. In the same way, AC electricity flows away from the power source to where the power is used. It is more straightforward to transmit AC over long distances, and it is the form of electricity that is in every household.

The other type of electricity, DC, has a continuous charge, and the voltage remains more or less stable. Instead of a wave, it is flat. DC is more stable, particularly at low voltage; therefore, many appliances and electronics use DC.

The next aspects of electricity that we will cover are that of voltage, current, and resistance:

Voltage is measured in volts and is defined as the potential difference between two points. For example, in a car battery, the potential difference between the positive and negative terminal is 12 Volts. Voltage is the driving force behind electricity. One volt is the potential difference between two points on a wire, where one ampere of current dissipates one watt of power. This may sound confusing, but it will make sense once we cover the other aspects.

- The voltage, or potential difference, is the driving force pushing the electrons from one point to another, and the term used to describe this flow of charge is termed as the current. Thus, the current describes the rate of flow of charge from one point to another.

- The ampere, or amp for short, is the measure of current flow in electricity. In order for electricity to flow, there needs to be an exchange of electrons from one point to another. This essentially means that there is a flow of charged particles from one point to another, which is electricity.

- The next term to look into is resistance. Resistance is measured in ohms, and it resists the flow of current due to a potential difference. If it weren't for resistance in materials, we would have perfect conductors and no electricity losses. Resistance essentially takes the energy that is transmitted via electricity and wastes some of it, typically in the form of heat.

A simple way to understand the concept of these three interacting aspects of electricity is to use an analogy of something that is easier to visualize than electricity. The most common and most straightforward analogy used is that of water flowing through a pipe. In terms of water moving through a pipe, voltage is the pressure of the water, the current is the flow rate, and the diameter of the pipe is the resistance. The higher the pressure is, the faster the flow rate will be. Similarly, if there is a higher potential difference or a larger voltage, there will be an increased flow of current. The voltage would be an increase of water pressure, resulting in increased water flow given the right conditions. Do not get confused when seeing the description of potential difference and voltage used interchangeably in datasheets and other documentation, as they are the same thing when referring to electricity. However, the diameter of the pipe will limit the flow of water. A more narrow pipe represents a higher resistance. In this instance, higher pressure is required for the same flow rattan to a setup with a wider diameter pipe.

The next concept that needs to be presented is that of electrical power. Power is measured in watts and is determined by the current and voltage of a system. To calculate the power, you only need to multiply the current and the voltage. The power determines how much energy is being transferred from the source to the load at any given time. For example, if a 12 V battery is driving a 2 A current across a load, then the power delivered to the load is the two multiplied by each other, or 24 W.

The Difference Between Power and Energy

The power measured in watts describes how much energy is used up at any given time, so when you see a light bulb that is 100 W, you know that it uses more energy every second than a 60 W light bulb. Total energy use is calculated by multiplying the power supplied in one moment by the amount of time power was supplied. However, this is different from how most energy meters work. When you receive an electrical bill, the amount of energy you use is not given to you in the units of energy, which is joules. It seems unusual that you aren't charged for the exact amount of energy you used, so why is that?

The short answer is that it is too complicated to measure the power flow at every single instance and determine its energy. Instead, what is used is referred to as watt-hours (Wh). When you are charged from your utility, the bill will typically describe the energy used up as kilowatt hours (kWh). A kilo represents a unit of 1,000, so 1,000 Wh is the same as 1 kWh. We are all charged in kWh from the utility because this is an average amount of energy that we use and not the precise amount itself. Typically, energy meters sample the amount of power being used once every 15 minutes. This means that four samples are taken over the span of an hour, and they all contribute to the overall amount of energy estimated (Enphase, n.d.).

An analogy to describe the difference between watts and watt-hours, which is essentially the difference between power and energy, is looking at speed and distance. Power is the rate of flow of energy, just as speed is the rate of change of distance. So, if you are driving at 60 mph, that would be equivalent to the power. If you were to drive for 30 minutes at this speed in a single direction, then you should cover 30miles, and this would be the equivalent of the energy. The faster you go, the more distance you can cover. Similar to the higher power you have, the more energy you can transfer.

When it comes to batteries, the measurement of energy available is typically provided in ampere-hours (Ah). This, again, can be translated into energy, as energy is the product of power and time. If, for example, you have a car battery, which is typically 12 V, and are given a rating of 200 Ah as the battery rating, then you can determine the energy stored by multiplying amp hours by the voltage, so 200 x 12, which is 6,000 Wh of 6 kWh of energy. The reason for this type of measurement is that it makes it easier to determine how long your batteries last. If you have the same 200 Ah battery and have several devices that you wish to power from it, you only need to look at how much current these devices draw to know how long the battery will last. For example, if you have lights and some devices connected to plugs and you work out that you will need 20 A of current, you only need to determine how much power you can draw from the battery. Theoretically, a battery being rated at 200 Ah should be able to supply 20 A for 10 hours. This will be covered in more detail in Chapter 2 when we discuss deep cycles for batteries.

Another important feature of electrical systems is protection. Protection is self-explanatory, and multiple protection devices are used to protect both people and electrical devices. Examples of protection devices are circuit breakers and fuses. When there is an electrical fault or a short circuit, these protection devices will be activated—circuit breakers trip to isolate the power to prevent any further damage or harm done to people. Think of them as a light switch that turns the power off automatically when it detects too much current flow to the load. When it comes to fuses, they will burn out instantly to open the circuit and stop the current from flowing when there is too much current flowing through them. Both fuses and circuit breakers typically have a rating that tells you how much current they will allow to flow through them and when they will operate to protect the electrical devices.

BASICS ON SOLAR SYSTEMS

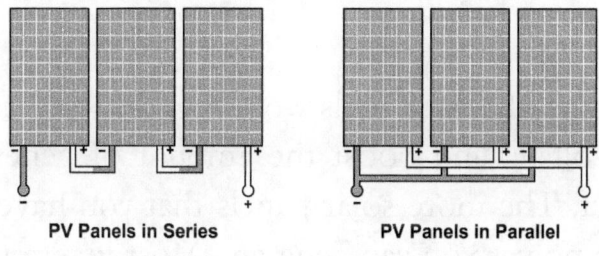

PV Panels in Series   PV Panels in Parallel

Now that we have covered some of the basic electricity terms, let's take a closer look at solar systems in particular and all the required components. You can connect panels to form what is called a string. A string of panels is typically made up of several panels connected in series. In electricity, the two main ways of connecting a circuit are called series-connected and parallel-connected components. A series connection links one component to another to form a big loop, whereas a parallel connection links components together like the steps of a ladder. All components are connected to the same line on each side.

When you connect a string of solar panels, if you opt for a DC charge controller, it is important to have fuses at the point of connection to the inverter and charge controller of the batteries. These fuses will protect the inverter, battery charger, and other solar panels if there is a short circuit.

Strings of solar panels work together to increase the voltage and boost the amount of generated power. The more solar panels that you have, the more power you can generate. Most inverters are equipped with multiple inputs from the solar panels to allow several strings of panels to be connected.

There is also certain terminology that you will need to be familiar with regarding electrical infrastructure relating to your solar system. The first of these things is a distribution board (DB). This is basically where your power is distributed to the different loads. All houses have a DB with an incomer from the utility, metering of some kind for the utility to track and charge you for your electricity usage, and feeders that feed power to your home's different areas. The concept is the same for an off-grid solar system. All your AC power will have to be fed from this single location. DBs typically have an incomer from your power source, which will be your inverter in this case. The incomer is typically a circuit breaker that is often called your main breaker. You will then find smaller circuit breakers that feed the different areas that require power. Lights are usually fed from what is known as a single-pole circuit breaker, and plugs, geysers, stoves, and other major loads are fed from double pole circuit breakers. A double pole circuit breaker has both a live and neutral connection from the circuit breaker to the loads, whereas single pole circuit breakers only have the live connection.

There is also typically an earth leakage unit that is designed to protect from earth faults in your system, an earth bar, a neutral bar, and a protected neutral bar. An earth leakage device is a device that is designed to protect you from getting electrocuted. It detects the current flowing to a load and returning from it, as electricity has to circulate in a loop. If it is detected that the current flowing to your loads does not match the current flowing back from them, it is assumed that there is a discharge to earth through a person or device. This is hazardous and could potentially injure a person, so when this situation is detected, the power is isolated completely. A DB is sometimes called a fuse box or feeder panel depending on the size and functionality, but they refer to the same fundamental thing.

An inverter is a device that converts the DC power that is generated from your solar system or batteries into AC power for you to use for plug points, appliances, and lighting. They are one of the core components of your solar system, alongside the batteries, battery charger, and solar panels. Inverters make use of semiconductive devices, and they have a limit to their efficiency. Be careful when sizing your solar system, as the power generated by your solar panels will not be 100% available for you to use in your AC system. A good rule of thumb to use is to take an efficiency of 85%, meaning that, of the power generated by your solar panels, only 85% will be available to use. This will help you avoid any issues in the future when you realize that you aren't able to get as much power out of your solar system as you originally expected.

When it comes to solar systems, there is a term known as peak sun hours (PSH), which effectively allows you to calculate how much power you can get from your solar panels on an average day. Although there may be 12 hours of sunlight on an average day, you may only have a listing of seven hours of PSH, as your panels will not be generating 100% power over the full 12 hours. Instead, there may be five hours of fully efficient production of electricity and four hours of partial efficiency, resulting in only seven hours of full productivity. In the four hours of partial sun exposure, you may get approximately 50% of the sun intensity and photons you would receive during the middle of the day. This means that the four hours of 50% sun intensity translate to two hours of PSH.

When you determine the amount of power that you can get from your panels, you shouldn't use the number of hours of sunlight during the day, but, rather, the number of PSH. This is also important for seasonal changes as your panels will inevitably have fewer PSH during the winter months when compared to the summer months.

Another concept that isn't often discussed is the power factor. Power is technically measured as apparent power, also known as active power, which makes up the watts that we are now familiar with, and the second type of power is known as reactive power. Reactive power is a power that doesn't show active use and is a part of your power that you want to reduce as far as possible. All inductive loads, such as stoves and geysers, have a component of inductance that demands reactive power. This power isn't obviously shown in your active power or watt usage, making it confusing sometimes when you look at your power demand and solar system capability and see a gap between the two. It's not easy to explain, but the basics are that a voltage is set up, and the current follows it. The greater the lag between the voltage set up and the flow of current is determined by induction, and the further behind the current lags, the lower your power factor and the more power is lost without delivering useful energy. The most typical way that reactive power is compensated for is by using filter devices such as capacitors. They are commonly used in larger-scale electrical systems but are costly and are not used often in residential applications.

Solar inverters are designed to supply your load based on its requirements. If you have large inductive loads, the chances are that you will have what is known as a poor power factor. Power factor is basically a ratio between the different forms of power. A typical load will have a power factor ranging from 0 to 1.0. A value of 1.0 is outstanding. It means that your ratio of apparent power, measured in volt-amps (VA), is exactly equal to your active, or real, power with a ratio of one to one. It may seem confusing since the ratio is not linear and is a root mean squared ratio. That being said, a power factor of 0.8 is terrible, whereas a power factor of 0.95 is very good. This translates to 80% of your power being used in a useful way versus 95% of your power being used in a useful way.

This is an important aspect to cover because your inverters will put out power to cater to loads of a certain size, but that doesn't consider the type of load you are connecting. If you are unaware of this theory, then you may end up underestimating the size of your inverter, expecting it to power loads that it simply isn't adequate for. No system will have a perfect power factor; thus, a lot of the power that your inverter will generate goes into this "wasted" energy that hasn't been accounted for. When configuring your inverter, you will typically be able to see the amount of real and reactive power that you are generating but not be able to compensate for this. There are devices known as power factor correction banks, but these are designed more for larger-scale systems.

In terms of power factor for your solar system, just assume that it accounts for a reduction in efficiency between the power that your inverter can generate and the power demand of your load. In this way, it will not take you by surprise later on when you aren't getting out what you expected.

There is also an aspect known as insulation. The insulation of a material is the opposite of the conductivity. If something is a good insulator, then it is a very poor conductor and vice versa. This is specific to electricity in this case, as conductivity could be for several other things, such as heat. It is important to have good insulation materials for things that should not be live. This includes the insulation material that surrounds cables and all components that shield you from live conductors. How well a material can withstand and protect you from live conductors is known as the insulation voltage rating. This is different for AC and DC voltages, as explained below.

How Inverters Work

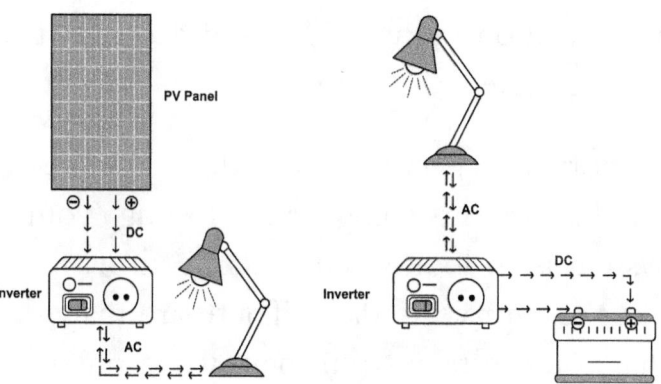

The process of converting DC power into AC power is known as inverting the power. The process of converting AC power into DC power is termed rectifying the power. When the process takes place, the voltage that you get on one side does not match the other side, i.e., 1 V of AC power does not become 1 V of DC power once it has been rectified. This is true for both the rectifying and inverting process. The DC voltage equivalent from rectifying AC can be calculated with the following simple equation:

Voltage Insulation Rating (DC) = Voltage Insulation Rating (AC) / 2

This implies that an insulation material that can protect you from 1,000V of AC power can only protect you from 700 V of DC power. It's important to know this difference so that you don't specify an insulator or any equipment with an insulation rating in AC and expect it to work for the same DC voltage.

Another aspect to consider with designing, purchasing, installing, and testing your solar system is to look at engineering firms that carry out these projects daily. There are many lessons that you can take from them when building your own system. It's easier to learn from other's mistakes or best practices than to have to go through the trouble yourself. One practice that is often skipped in do-it-yourself projects is having a design review of some kind. If you have designed your own system, you may not be aware of any gaps in your design or things that you may not have considered that are commonplace in solar systems. Engineering companies will hold internal reviews where a team of experts gives feedback on one person's design. The design will be scrutinized to determine whether the solution makes sense technically, legally, ethically, that it meets quality standards, and that it is, indeed, the best fit solution for the requirements at hand. A good idea is to discuss your design with someone who has carried out their own solar system before and get input. It can be expanded into getting multiple opinions on your design and plans. It isn't about changing your design completely because someone else has a different opinion on how you should do things. It is more of a guideline to help you think laterally and think of things that may have slipped through the cracks when you carried out the design of your system. Again, it is far easier and cheaper to make changes to your design before it has materialized than after!

Chapter 3: How To Choose The Right Battery

When it comes to figuring out which battery to use for your solar system, you need to know what different batteries are available on the market and the pros and cons of the different types of batteries. You may think you are getting a great deal on cheap batteries only to find that they don't perform well and only last you two to three years before failing. You may look at the price tag of a high-end battery and feel as though you are being ripped off only to find that it is a deep cycle battery that performs well and lasts you over ten years. It's all about selecting the best option for the right price.

It's important to remember, once again, that the cost of something isn't purely about the price tag that you see when you first purchase something. The cost of ownership should also be compared. If you have a maintenance-free battery, then you will save on maintenance costs. Also, if you have an expensive battery option that lasts you ten years and another is half the cost but only lasts for three years, you will save in the long run by going for the more expensive battery.

Let's begin by explaining what a deep cycle battery is. Batteries are basically devices that store energy. They require charging in order to absorb the energy. When this power is needed, the batteries discharge to supply the power. The process of charging and discharging is not perfect, and there are losses experienced. Due to the physical construction of batteries, they cannot be discharged to 0% charge. Standard batteries can only discharge to 60% charge, meaning that only 40% of the energy stored in the batteries can be accessed. Deep cycle batteries can discharge 80% of their stored energy, which is significantly more than standard batteries. However, in order to ensure that the lifespan of the batteries is per manufacturer specifications, you shouldn't discharge them beyond a 45% charge. If you stick to this, you will be able to use the batteries for a much longer time. When you discharge the battery to its limit, there is internal degradation of the batteries, which means that they will never be able to store as much energy as before. The more you cycle beyond the point specified, the more degradation will occur until the batteries will not be able to charge at all. This will inevitably happen with all batteries, but it is better to have batteries last for five years than overwork them and last only three years (Crown Battery, 2018).

When it comes to deep cycle batteries, you can cycle the charge and discharge amounts at a much higher rate than other battery types. Most batteries will also have a rated number of cycles guaranteed, which is an important factor to take into consideration when selecting a battery. Some will guarantee up to 500 cycles, which would result in less than two years of daily use. Others will guarantee as many as 2,500 cycles, meaning they will last you much longer even if you are discharging them more than once per day (Energy Matters, n.d.).

Two additional categories describe the different types of deep cycle batteries. These are sealed type, or maintenance-free batteries, and flooded deep cycle batteries. Flooded deep cycle batteries require inspection and maintenance. For lead-acid batteries, which are the most commonly used, there is a minimum and maximum level of electrolytic liquid. When the liquid drops below the minimum level, they need to be topped up with distilled water. Many batteries are described as sealed type batteries, but aren't truly sealed batteries. This is specifically true for absorbed glass mat (AGM) batteries, which are actually valve regulated and not truly sealed. In fact, most sealed type batteries are actually valve regulated. As another example, lead acid batteries give off hydrogen gas over time, specifically when they charge, and this gas builds up pressure in the batteries. This is why, instead of being completely sealed, these batteries have a valve to allow the gas to be released before the internal pressure gets to a dangerous level.

There are also different types of batteries that work using different principles. The most common types of batteries used for energy storage are lithium-ion, flooded lead-acid, AGM, and gel batteries. Each of these primary types of batteries have pros and cons, which are essential to know for you to decide what will best fit your requirements.

Lithium-Ion Batteries

Lithium-ion batteries are one of the most commonly used batteries used today. They are lightweight compared to other batteries, which explains why they are used in many electronic devices such as cell phones, tablets, and laptops. They are incredibly durable and are more resilient to harsh weather conditions than other batteries.

They also last the longest of the five battery types mentioned above, and they require very little or no maintenance at all. The batteries themselves are sealed, so it is mostly the connections that need to be checked once in a while to see if the battery is still charging and discharging adequately. The batteries are also compact and don't take up a lot of space, which is great when this is a factor to consider, such as in an RV or on a boat.

The disadvantage when it comes to lithium-ion batteries is that they are costly. A typical, deep-cycle lithium-ion battery will cost about four times as much as the other options that will be discussed. That being said, they will last the longest out of all of the batteries, with many being rated to last between 10 and 15 years. Another drawback with lithium-ion batteries is that they are sensitive to electrical faults and need to be protected against them, particularly voltage surges. They are also sensitive to temperature and will not last as long in high temperatures (above 25 degrees Celsius, or 77 degrees Fahrenheit). This means that they need to be stored in a cool, dry area to maximize their lifespan. Another issue comes with disposing of lithium-ion batteries. If a lithium-ion battery is pierced, it can be explosive. This is why manufacturers of lithium-ion batteries take every precaution possible to ensure any failure is sealed by having protective plates. However, if these batteries were to end up in a dump, the risk increases. This means that, after the batteries stop working, there is a small expense for specialists to dispose of them responsibly.

FLOODED LEAD ACID BATTERIES

The next battery that we will look at is the flooded lead acid battery. As previously mentioned, they do require regular inspection and maintenance. They have been around for a long time and are known to be reliable hence car batteries today still make use of lead acid batteries. They are also used in battery tripping units in almost every substation in the world for backup power to protect devices connecting the grid.

One of the most significant advantages of these types of batteries is that they can supply a large amount of power quickly without damage to the batteries. If you turn on a device with an element such as a kettle, geyser, or toaster, the power drawn spikes as a large amount of current is needed to power these devices. These batteries are able to supply this demand without it affecting the quality of the power being delivered. They are also cheap in comparison to the other types of batteries on this list. If you have several different large loads that you will be turning on and off regularly, these batteries may be the option you are looking for. Although these batteries require maintenance, they have a relatively simple design and are easy to repair.

The disadvantage with these batteries is that they contain a liquid with a cap keeping the liquid in, but they need to be kept upright, and it is not advisable to move them often. Although they typically have a cap to keep the liquid from spilling over, it is not a vacuum seal, and the electrolytic liquid will leak if the batteries are moved often. Also, as mentioned, they require frequent inspection and topping up with distilled water when the electrolytic liquid drops below the minimum threshold. They also have a low energy density, meaning that they don't store a large amount of energy for their physical size and weight. This type of battery also gives off hydrogen gas as they charge, which is flammable. This isn't a problem when they are stored in an area with good ventilation, but if they are stored in a sealed room, the buildup of hydrogen can be dangerous.

These batteries also have the risk of chemical burns as they do contain acid. It is crucial that these batteries are stored upright so as not to leak this acidic electrolytic liquid. The term "electrolytic", for the liquid contained in batteries, is used because these batteries use a process known as electrolysis to store a charge. When the batteries are charging, electrolysis occurs, which converts the chemicals into ions and anions, which are the batteries' positive and negatively charged elements. These then combine to form a single compound, and this process is used to store and release energy. Chemical processes require energy. In certain chemical processes, energy is released when different elements combine. This change of energy levels is what is analyzed when determining what compounds could potentially make for good batteries. Other conditions are considered as well when selecting what chemicals to make use of in batteries. Such as the chemical process taking place at room temperature, how easy it is to reverse the process, and whether or not degradation can be minimized so the chemical process can be reversed and repeated many times. Batteries are chemical reactions in a mostly closed system and store and release energy in the form of electricity when we require it.

There is also the risk of thermal runaway where the batteries are overused and overheat, which results in dangerously high temperatures for the electrolytic material. This is an extremely infrequent occurrence, and battery manufacturers design their batteries to reduce this risk as far as practically possible. If your batteries are not operating correctly and are running hot, then it is highly recommended that you remove them from the operation. This rare occurrence will occur when there is a defect in a battery; therefore, if this were to happen to one of your batteries, it would likely only be in one of the batteries in your battery bank. A warranty claim can almost always be made in this instance, provided you are storing your batteries correctly and in accordance with the manufacturer's specifications.

Valve Regulated or Sealed Batteries

The final battery is the valve regulated, or sealed, battery. These come in two main forms: AGM and gel type batteries. Unlike the flooded lead acid batteries, these units are self-contained and require no real maintenance, only an inspection from time to time. The most significant advantage of these batteries is that they can hold their charge for a very long time, unlike most batteries which discharge over time. Think of a car that has been standing for a few weeks, but it still has enough charge to start the car. That ability to hold charge while not being used over extended periods of time is a massive benefit with these batteries. This makes them ideal for solar systems that aren't used daily, such as in RVs. They are self-contained and give off only trace amounts of hydrogen over time. They are also significantly cheaper than lithium-ion batteries, which are also sealed batteries that do not spill. The final advantage of these batteries is that they are non-hazardous, making them safer to dispose of than lithium-ion batteries.

One of the disadvantages associated with these batteries is that they are more expensive than flooded lead acid batteries. They also don't last as long as lithium-ion batteries, resulting in their demand decreasing over time. They are bulkier than lithium-ion batteries and have a shorter lifespan.

AGM batteries, in particular, are incredibly robust and can handle movement and shock. This is why they are used as car batteries in almost all internal combustion engine vehicles. These batteries can also charge to a full charge at a lower voltage than specified. This means that even a 12 V rated battery can be fully charged with a 10 V supply voltage, which is hugely advantageous. They can also handle the high current without being damaged. AGM batteries can be charged quicker than other batteries and can give a deep cycle discharge when power is needed. This makes them just as popular as lithium-ion batteries for solar solutions, especially when it comes to mobile applications such as RV's, boats, and trailers for camping.

Gel batteries, like AGM batteries, are robust and resistant to shock and are also maintenance-free apart from inspections. They also have the advantage of not leaking even if their physical construction is compromised. They are incredibly resilient in extreme temperatures, making them functional even in extreme weather conditions, such as low or high temperatures, high humidity, or high altitude. These batteries can be transported without issues and operate normally, even when on their side or upside down. Because of their extreme resilience to extreme weather, they are often used in marine and aircraft applications.

However, gel batteries are not as popular when it comes to solar solutions because they are far more expensive than AGM batteries with similar properties. They are also extremely sensitive to how they are charged and can be damaged easily electrically, despite being robust physically. They also don't cycle as deeply as other batteries and are large and heavy for the amount of energy they can store.

The Takeaway

The two most advantageous battery options to consider for your solar solution are lithium-ion batteries and AGM batteries. They are the two most prominent players in the market because they are better suited for off-grid solar systems than the other battery types.

Of course, the capital expenditure on these batteries is constantly changing, but, at present, AGM batteries cost between US$300 and US$500 for a 12V, 200Ah unit. In comparison, lithium-ion batteries with similar ratings will cost between US$1,200 and US$1,500. This clearly shows the advantage of AGM batteries from a cost-saving perspective, but the trade-off comes with the depth of discharge and number of cycles that the batteries are capable of. AGM batteries for this price will typically be able to discharge and charge around 400 times, while lithium-ion batteries can discharge approximately 2,000 times. Although the AGM batteries are a third of the price, the lithium-ion batteries will last five times as long.

Chapter 4: How To Choose The Right Solar Panel

Choosing the right solar panel for you may seem a bit daunting, especially in an age where there are more options than we know what to do with. In order to figure out what will work best for you, you need to ask a few questions so you can decide for yourself. There is so much information available online and in the market, so it is helpful to know what to look out for and what to avoid when making your decision. Everyone has an opinion on what's best for you, and worse than that is someone in sales trying to sell a specific product to you. Unfortunately, all salespeople will want to sell a product that they have, so you need to take what they say with a grain of salt. You should be informed of the positives and negatives of any solar panel option, as the salesperson for a specific panel will not give you the negatives that their solar panel has.

Solar panels are all rated according to standard test conditions (STC). This means that all ratings you will find listed on solar panel datasheets for performing and are expected to perform are provided at STC levels. This includes a temperature of 25 degrees Celsius, or 77 degrees Fahrenheit; an altitude at sea level, or less than 1,000m or 3,280 ft; low levels of humidity; and an average amount of solar radiation reaching the earth. Solar radiation intensity determines just how much energy is available at any given location to convert into electricity via the photovoltaic process.

The average used is 1,000 W per square meter. This means that for every square meter of space, or just under 11 square feet, there is 1,000 W of potential power available to convert to electricity using standard PV solar panels, regardless of what type. This is the rating according to direct solar radiation, which is added to via indirect solar radiation. This includes all reflected light off of other surfaces, including pavements and buildings, which increases solar radiation levels by a small amount. This level differs from one location to another depending on the amount of sunlight received in that place.

The amount of solar radiation that is available to you is determined by your geographical location. There are online resources available that indicate the intensity of solar radiation for every place on earth. NASA is to thank for a lot of this data that is available to us. Many locations are fortunate to have a much higher solar radiation available per unit area, and can generate a lot more power with the same number of panels than locations with average solar radiation levels. However, many of these areas also experience high average daily temperatures, which results in the de-rating of the solar panel's ability to generate power. In many instances, these two factors balance out and the benefits of a higher solar radiation intensity don't impact the solar power generation levels of these solar arrays. This means that a desert-mounted solar panel cannot necessarily generate more power than a rooftop installation in France. It's all about associating your solar radiation levels with temperature and where you are in making use of this solar system. If you experience very little direct sunlight, you are likely to draw a much lower level of energy from your solar panels than people living in high solar radiation areas.

Solar panels will generate the most amount of electricity when they are directly facing the sun. This essentially maximizes the surface area of the panels that can be exposed to photons. This means that when you install your solar panels, it is beneficial to have them exposed to the most amount of sunlight throughout the day. Apart from shadows and other potential obstructions that could reduce the amount of sunlight received by the panels, the angle at which you mount them is crucial. This is determined by what is known as the azimuth. The azimuth describes the angle at which the sun rises and sets on the east to west path. Your latitude will change the sun's angle in the sky, and you will want to tilt your panels to face the sun at the highest rate possible. This means that, in the northern hemispheres, such as in the US, your angles will be tilted to face more towards the south rather than lying flat. The opposite is experienced for locations in the southern hemisphere. The general rule of thumb is to take your coordinates, more specifically your latitude, and add 15 degrees for summer and subtract 15 degrees for winter. This is for situations where you intend to adjust the tilt angle of your solar panels from season to season. This action will not affect your energy generation capacity by more than 5%; therefore, many people opt to mount their solar systems at the same latitude angle on a rigid mounting structure and do not adjust between seasons (De Rooij, 2020).

The key is to narrow down your selection so that you know what makes sense and what doesn't. If you want to install a permanent installation on the roof of your home, then your requirements will vary from if you want to put up a few panels on an RV to power you as you take a road trip.

The first thing that you need to ask yourself is what your application will be. Will you have a fixed solar installation in the same set location, such as on the roof of your home, or a mobile solar system on a car, boat, RV, or camping trailer. Think of this as a mobile or non-mobile solution moving forward. The mobile solution needs to be durable and robust enough to handle vibration and other mechanical shocks without being damaged. Non-mobile solutions do not need to be as resilient to vibration, but will need to be strong enough to handle various weather conditions, such as hail storms, without being damaged.

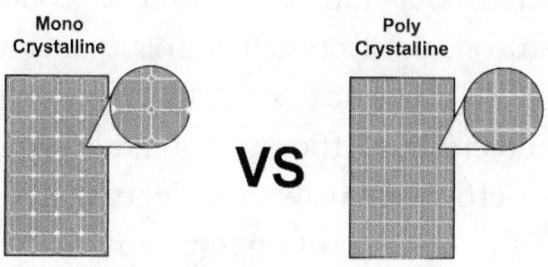

There are two predominant divisions of solar panels available on the market today. They are monocrystalline and polycrystalline. The difference between these two options is in their manufacturing. Monocrystalline solar cells are manufactured from a single silicon crystal, whereas polycrystalline panels are manufactured from several silicon crystals combined. This means that monocrystalline panels are much more expensive because they require a lot more manufacturing finesse in order to keep them uniform. This leads to them being more energy-efficient but a lot more expensive. Over 90% of the solar panels installed today are polycrystalline because they are around 80% as efficient in capturing energy, but they are far cheaper. A typical monocrystalline solar panel will have an energy capturing capacity of around 25%, making them the most efficient solar panel per unit area. They are mostly used in installations where space is limited, but the price isn't a concern. In comparison, a polycrystalline solar panel will have a typical efficiency of 20%, making them substantially less efficient but far cheaper. This level of efficiency may sound extremely low, but that is the amount of energy captured from the sun per unit area, and that number is growing as the materials and technology we apply improve over time.

Rigid and Flexible Solar Panels

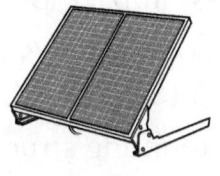
Rigid Solar Panels with adjustable mount

Flexible Solar Panel installed on car roof

There are also flexible and rigid solar panel options. Rigid solar panels are designed to be installed as they are on rooftops or mounted in such a way that their bulky structure is not intrusive. Flexible solar panels are designed to be lightweight and compact so that they can streamline a design. This is why flexible solar panels are used in cars and boats more often than in other applications. Once again, they make up a very small market segment because they are considerably more costly. They are also more susceptible to damage from impact, whereas rigid solar panels are designed to be more robust.

Let's take a look at a rooftop installation on an RV as an example to weigh the pros and cons of using a rigid or flexible solar solution. The immediate and obvious advantage of using flexible solar panels over rigid ones in this installation is that they are much lighter and won't weigh the vehicle down. Another massive advantage is that they don't require a bulky frame to mount the panels on and have much less impact on the vehicle's fuel efficiency, as they don't all have a lot of drag. In comparison, rigid solar panels mounted on the roof require a mounting structure and are large panels themselves. These factors combined mean that there will be a lot more drag on the vehicle when driven, and the additional weight will further degrade fuel efficiency. Rigid panels are typically four to five times heavier than flexible panels.

The advantage of rigid solar panels is that they can be moved or adjusted in order to be directed towards the sun, maximizing the power generated. Flexible panels are typically mounted flush to the surface of a vehicle, which means that you cannot adjust the angle of the panels to face the sun directly. Fortunately, there is a technology that is present for flexible solar panels. This is basically raised dots on the panel to improve the solar capturing capability of the panels. However, this is still less effective than simply aiming the panel to face the sun directly, which is more practical than the rigid panels.

The rigid solar panels are very durable, so they are more resistant to scratches to the panels from things like branches. This means that flexible panels are more likely to get damaged in this way than rigid solar panels. The option you pick is purely based on your requirement and budget, as both of these panel types are tried and tested in multiple industries.

In terms of permanently installed panels that will not be moved, such as on houses or panels that are moved to a location and positioned, such as camping trailers, the energy generated per unit area is critical. Many solar panels are 2m long and 1m wide, or roughly 6.5 ft long and 3.5 ft wide, with varying energy generation capabilities. Some of these units will be rated at 250 W, and others at 400 W. It is beneficial to use panels that have a higher energy density, which means that they can generate more power per unit area. These panels are made up of higher efficiency cells, or energy cells that are packed more tightly on a solar panel and hence can generate more power per unit area (Matasci, 2019).

Every solar panel is made up of a string of solar cells that are connected together. Because these cells are typically connected together in series, they all need to be operational for the solar panel to generate power. If there is an open circuit between cells, then the panel will not generate electricity.

Many panels have built-in components to try and minimize this risk and still generate some power even if there is damage to one of the cells. For this same reason, solar panels will lose power generated when there is shading. It only takes one cell out of dozens, of which there are typically 72 but can be as high as 96, being in a shadow to reduce the power generated by the entire solar panel. This is because less current is permitted to flow in the entire panel, which can drop the power output by as much as 60%. It is a huge issue to have shading on your solar panel if even a tiny portion of the panel can result in such a huge loss in power generation. Again, there are technologies available to reduce the impact of partial shading on solar panels, but this comes with additional cost. Many solar panels have built-in diodes and other devices which manage power loss far better than standard solar panels. If you run the risk of your solar panels being partly shaded regularly, such as from trees around the solar system, it is worth looking into these types of solar panels.

Always be sure to look out for brands that are internationally accredited. There is no use in bargaining on a solar panel that seems to be of a price that is too good to be true. Suppose the main brands that you recognize, such as CanadaSolar, Jinko, or Trina, are far more expensive than another brand. In that case, it is likely a scam or a product that hasn't met international standards. As with all things in technology, inferior products will not last long, and you will end up wasting your money and have to upgrade later to the units with a standard price.

The most common symbols to look out for on a product to ensure it meets international safety or quality standards are the CE or UL marks. The CE mark stands for "Conformitè Europëenne," European body that confirms that a product meets the body's requirements in terms of safety and quality. Products manufactured or distributed in Europe have to have this marking to represent the quality. In the USA, however, these markings are not compulsory for products being distributed. Many manufacturers still opt to put these symbols on their products to sell their products as good quality products. The UL symbol stands for "Underwriters Laboratories," which indicates that Underwriters Laboratories has inspected samples of the product. They have determined that it conforms to their safety standards. When you are looking for panels to purchase for your solar system, always look for these symbols. Stick to the products that show these labels to know that you are getting a product that has been scrutinized and was found to be safe.

When selecting a solar panel type, you will need to look at what is readily available from solar panel suppliers where you plan to purchase the panels. There are often shortages of a specific size due to large projects buying up all of the availability of certain panels. There are multiple brands that you can choose from, and you will often find that a large order has been placed which hasn't been fully collected, or an excess of panels was ordered for a large client. This could lead to excellent deals and discounted costs on certain panel types. At this stage, it's important for you to look at whether the availability and cost of panels on the market matches the design that you have put together for your solar system. If you specified polycrystalline, 360 W panels, but there is an excellent price for polycrystalline, 320 W panels, then it may be worthwhile to go for the cheaper option, even if you do lose out on some of the power output from each panel. Go back to your original design and see whether this change in panel selection will have an impact, especially if you have to purchase more panels than you had initially intended.

Electrical systems also tend to have a rating that decreases when you go above an altitude of 1,000 m, or 3,280 ft, above sea level. This may impact your installation if you plan to install or make use of it above this level. The same goes for temperature and humidity. Solar panels have a derating above 25 degrees Celsius or 77 degrees Fahrenheit. The depreciation is linear up until approximately 75 degrees Celsius or 167 degrees Fahrenheit. Suppose you experience high temperatures during the summer months. In that case, you may experience a derating factor and only end up generating 90% of the possible power output of the solar panels themselves. It is crucial to consult the specific solar panel datasheet that you plan on using in order to see these values and be realistic in specifying your system.

Solar panels also deteriorate over time due to the photovoltaic effect. Typical panels are tagged with a lifespan of 25 years, and, at that point, they will only be able to generate 40% of the power they were originally rated for. This deterioration is also approximately linear over time, so even after ten years of operation, your panels will only generate around 80% of the power they were in year one. A solar system is a long-term investment, so having this information is important when looking far into the future at the benefits that come from making use of them. It's not to say that after 25 years the solar panels will not continue working for many years after that. It is more relevant to power generation plants that use tens of thousands of solar panels. This loss of possible revenue makes the solar plant non-profitable after 25 years if the panels aren't completely replaced. You could still have a solar system on your house working after 40 years.

This rating is also a conservative average that manufacturers specify and does not equate to every single panel deteriorating at the same rate. There are many pros to using solar panels, but it requires that you fully understand the current limitations of the products in the market today.

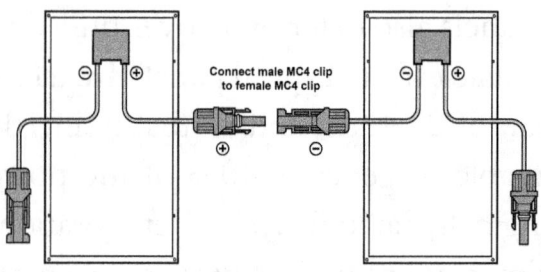

When connecting solar panels to form a string, you will need connecting wires and clips, most commonly the MC4 clips, which have a male and female connection and clip tightly when pushed together. Most solar panels are manufactured to have short lengths of wires, with one wire connected with a male clip and another with a female clip. This makes it easier to discern between the positive and negative terminals. It is essential to connect the positive of one panel into the negative of the adjacent unit and form a string. If you connect a panel the wrong way around, then the voltages will cancel out, and it could damage the internal cells of the solar panel. Fortunately, most units have built-in diodes, which are electronic components that only allow current to flow in one direction and not the other. These diodes prevent current from flowing through one panel, keeping it from running through the entire string of panels.

When you are specifying a solar panel for your application, confirm that the solar panel has these wire leads with the MC4 clips on them. Also, make sure that the leads are long enough to reach between two panels that are mounted right next to each other. Older solar panel models were often supplied with a terminal box with a positive and negative connection point without these cable lengths, meaning that more materials would need to be purchased, and installing the units becomes more labor-intensive. There is no point in saving cost on your solar panels by selecting units without wire leads, known as tails, and ending up spending more when combining the cost of the wires, clips, and solar panels than a more expensive solar panel that comes with these components included.

The same goes for mounting clips. Something as small as having pre-drilled holes for mounting brackets to be used to secure your solar panels can save you time and expendable parts, such as drill bits. Modern solar panels come with an aluminum frame built around the cells. These frames typically have a lip, which means that they can be clamped to a structure and no drilling will be required for the solar panel itself. This maintains its integrity and reduces the risk of accidentally drilling through the protective glass and creating a weak spot in it. Be sure to look for solar panels with this frame if you have selected to use rigid solar panels.

Chapter 5: How To Choose The Right Wires, Fuses, and Inverter

Now that we have sized the solar system that you require, determined which batteries will suit your application, and established which solar panels will be the best fit, it's time to look at all the other major components you will require for your solar system. This chapter will focus on sizing and selecting your inverter, fuses for protection, and cables to connect the panels, inverter, battery, and loads. It will then expand this to typical mounting structures that are used for various applications. In Chapter 6, the process of installing and testing your solar system will be covered, so the mounting structures presented in this chapter are just to help you select the right units for your requirements.

Sizing Your Cables and Wires

To start, the cables that you use have a significant impact on your solar system. There are specific single-core cables that are required to use for DC systems. Cables rated to handle 1,000 V of AC power aren't necessarily suited to use in DC circuits. When looking at cable options, make sure that you select one with a DC-rated voltage and ensure that the string of solar panels you have to connect to your inverter does not exceed this DC voltage. The current rating of the cable that you require is also extremely important. If you have a string of panels that will supply 10 A, then the cable you select needs to be rated at 10 A or higher. It is advisable to select a cable that is one size larger than the rated current that you require. This is to ensure that they can handle a short circuit current. Fortunately, with solar systems, the fault current is very close to the full load current of the solar panels. This is because they cannot supply excess power to a short circuit, unlike many other sources, such as generators.

Another consideration that you need to look at is the length of the cables from the solar panels to your inverter. The longer a cable is, the more internal resistance they have and the more power losses you will experience. There is a phenomenon known as voltage drop on cables due to length. Most solar systems are designed to have the inverter close to the panels, so your cable length shouldn't be long enough to create a voltage drop across them. When selecting an AC cable to be installed on the output of your inverter to a distribution board, this may be a consideration that you have to look at. We will cover this once we complete the requirements to consider in your DC cables.

When considering the type of cable you require, it's essential to think about the nature of the installation. Some cables are manufactured with protective armoring, which is useful for cables buried in the ground or mounted where they could experience an impact that risks cutting into the cable. The downside of an armored cable is that it is more expensive and more rigid. It's far easier to bend an unarmoured cable, making it easier to install. A word of caution here: All cables have a minimum bending radius. This means that if you need to bend a 90 degree angle in the cable, you have to bend it in a curve rather than put a 90 degree bend on the cable, as this will damage it and create a weak spot. All cables have this bending radius listed on a datasheet for reference. It's usually given in inches or millimeters and assists you in installing the cables according to the manufacturer's specifications.

Another consideration is in using cables that are resistant to ultraviolet (UV) light. The sun gives off UV light, and this can degrade cables over time. Cables that are not resistant to UV light will become hard and crack. If a crack goes from the outer cable to the live conductor inside, then you may experience a fault or risk being electrocuted if you touch this part of the cable. As all solar panels need to be mounted outdoors in order to capture the sunlight, selecting UV-resistant cables is recommended.

Most solar panels are manufactured with lengths of positive and negative cables with connector clips on them. These cable lengths are known as tails, and the cables that you select should connect to these tails. A lot of the time, solar panels have tails that are long enough to connect panels to either side of it to form the strings, and you only need to connect to the first and last panel in a string to connect it to the inverter. This saves cost on cables and connector clips. You will need to make sure that the cable you select will be able to fit the right connector clip on it to connect to the solar panel clips. These clips have a range of wire sizes that will fit them and are designed to fit into all the common cable sizes typically used in solar installations.

A typical cable that you could select would be a 2.5mm2, single-core, unarmoured, 1,000 voltage in direct current (VDC), UV resistant cable. Many datasheets are available from different cable manufacturers, including Aberdare and Lapp, among other known brand names. When it comes to your AC cable connecting from your inverter to a distribution board, the ratings you need to consider are very similar. The main difference is that AC has inductance as well as resistance, which combine to form impedance. Impedance is the same as resistance in a DC system, which is what restricts the flow of current and creates losses. It is similar to how drag creates air resistance that reduces the ability of vehicles to travel fast. Essentially, there are additional losses to consider with AC cables that aren't present in DC systems. Fortunately, these tend to be small, and you won't need to concern yourself with short cable runs.

How to Earth or Ground Your System

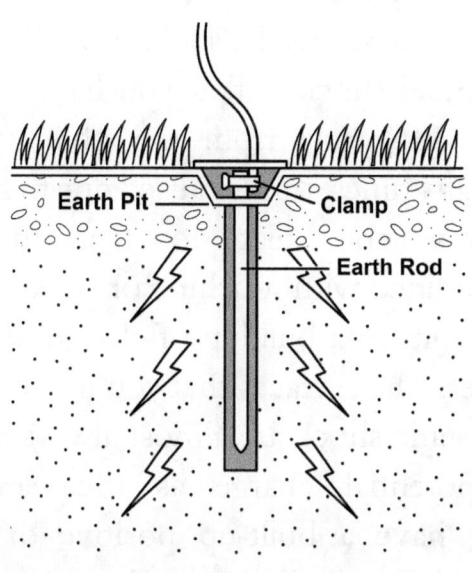

Another major consideration that many people neglect to address is the earthing of your solar system. Earthing, or grounding, refers to linking parts of your solar system to earth, making it safe. When it comes to earthing, one of the most important aspects to consider is known as equipotential. This means that different points have the same connection to the earth; therefore, no potential difference can exist between them, resulting in current flowing from one point to another, especially through a person. It is a critical safety feature that all electrical installations need to consider.

Picture a moment when you have touched something conductive, be it a door handle or car body, and you received a static shock. The reason for this small shock is that you have a different potential difference from the object that you touch. Many times, this is caused due to shoes that you wear which insulate you from the ground. This, combined with touching or rubbing various things, results in a buildup of charge of one type or another. The surfaces that you touch moments before a static shock are almost always neutral, at an equipotential charge as the earth. You, however, have a built-up positive or negative charge which will dissipate when you come in contact with the earth, resulting in a static shock. The purpose of equipotential earthing is to ensure that all non-live parts of an electrical system are at the same potential as earth, making them safe to touch one another. The other purpose of having equipotential earthing is that any earth fault will be detected and isolated. An earth fault means that a conductor carrying electricity has a connection to a component that should not be conducting electricity. If you have a toaster constricted by metal, then the last thing you want is for the entire toaster to become live and electrocute you if you touch it. Without equipotential earthing, you would not even realize that the toaster's body was live. With equipotential earthing and the correct earthing protection, as soon as a live wire touches the toaster's body from within, the equipotential bonding conductor leads that power to earth, resulting in a trip and isolation of electricity flowing to the toaster.

More than half of the faults that occur in electrical systems are due to earth faults or incorrect earthing, so it is a good starting point.

Consideration for Lightning Risks

Another major aspect of solar systems that you should consider is lightning protection. Lightning behaves in much the same way that static electricity behaves. There is a build up of charge between the clouds and the earth, resulting in a voltage that spirals until lightning results in a burst of current from one to the other, discharging the buildup of charge. The trouble with solar systems is that they act as a beacon for lightning. The myth that lightning strikes the highest point has some validity to it, but probably not in the way that you perceive it.

When you install your solar system, you should carry out a lightning risk assessment to know what type of protection you should install. The last thing you want is for your solar panels to be hit with a lightning strike, causing your solar system to need replacement. A typical lightning risk assessment uses the rolling sphere method to determine all the at-risk points of a lightning strike. At the end of the day, lightning is trying to reach equipotential earth. If there is an array of solar panels, then there are many areas where lightning may strike. This is where you need to install an equipotential lightning rod with its own dedicated link to earth. These lightning rods are not necessarily the massive poles that you see atop skyscrapers, but are relatively short lightning rods that are able to reduce the risk of lightning striking any one of the adjacent panels using the rolling sphere method.

Historically, lightning masts were specified according to a general rule. From the tip of the lightning rod, if you took a 45-degree angle down towards earth in all directions and drew an imaginary line down, that is the level of protection that it can offer. For example, if you had a 10 foot high lightning rod, it could only effectively protect against lightning strikes in a 10 foot radius around the rod. This method is still a good rule of thumb, but the improved method is known as the rolling sphere method. In this method, an imaginary sphere of a diameter determined by the level of protection required is rolled over your installation, and any point that it touches should be fitted with a lightning rod of a specific height. It sounds confusing, but imagine you have a beach ball and you roll it over a kitchen counter. Each point that it touches requires a lightning rod. Now imagine that a lightning rod is a mug placed where the ball first touches the counter. The beach ball now needs to roll over the mug. When the ball touches the counter again, you need another mug or lightning rod, and so on. By the end of rolling the beach ball over the counter, the mugs should prevent the ball from touching the counter altogether. This is like having lightning rods placed on a solar array. Instead of the lightning reaching your solar panels, like the beach ball not reaching the countertop, the lighting will strike the lightning rods, like the beach ball only touching the mugs.

The goal with solar systems is to have fewer lightning rods of lower height to reduce any impact from potential shading or obstructions due to having these rods stick out from your solar system. It is a cheap exercise to add these lightning arrestors, and they may well protect your panels, cables, inverter, and batteries from a catastrophic failure due to a lightning strike. Also, many insurance companies will insist that you have some form of lightning protection in order to cover your solar system or what your solar system is mounted on, such as a house. Insurance companies recognize the fire hazard that comes with a solar system, and you don't want to lose everything without any coverage.

All solar systems, especially those installed on houses, require an easily accessible kill switch. This is typically connected and mounted outside the vehicle or house so that, if there is a fire, flood, or another emergency, the solar system can be isolated from the outside without anyone having to risk their lives to go inside and risk electrocution or worse.

Specifying Your Inverter and Charge Controller

When it comes to the inverter that you select, the main criteria you need to consider is the power capacity of the inverter. If you determine that you will require 3 kW of power at any given time, you need to have an inverter to meet this demand. It is recommended that you select an inverter that is oversized for your current requirements in case you expand or need to add more load at a later stage. It is also important to figure out how many strings of solar panels can connect to your inverter. Some inverters may be rated for just a single string, while others will cater for two or three strings. This is also relevant to the system voltage of your solar system. Each panel that you add to your string will increase the DC voltage of the string. Inverters will have a maximum DC voltage rating for their input, and you cannot exceed this voltage. It would also be a waste not to make use of voltage to maximize your power generation capability. Inverters are rated with a specific power availability, and this requires both a voltage of a certain range and a current of a certain range. The best practice is to maximize your voltage as far as possible in order to get the power that you require. If the rated string voltage of an inverter is 120 Volts of DC power, then connecting a string rated at 48 Volts DC would reduce the power capability of the inverter. It is possible to expand in the future for such a consideration. Still, it would also be possible to expand the system by connecting a second string of panels in parallel to the first string that has been connected. This is typically determined by the configuration and connection of your combiner box or the rating of and number of DC inputs on your inverter.

Inverters also put out a high-pitched sound that, in some cases, falls into the audible range for humans. It's important to consult the inverter manual or, preferably, see a demo unit in action to avoid purchasing an inverter that gives off this noise, as it can be highly annoying and result in headaches over time. Most inverters will have an operational frequency rating that you can look at and compare to audible frequencies, which typically range from 20 Hertz to 20,000 Hertz for people with perfect hearing. Do not confuse this audible frequency range with the switching frequency of the semiconductive devices.

One of the most useful features of many modern-day off-grid inverters is that they are equipped with a charge controller built into the unit. This makes it a single device to connect your batteries, solar panels, and AC loads to via a DB. It makes the inverters a space and cost-saver in the long run. The inverter will be able to convert the DC power generated into AC power for your consumption when the sun is out. At the same time, the excess power generated will be used to charge your batteries via the inverter's built-in charge controller. This allows you to maximize the power that your solar panels generate and avoid wasting power. This system is streamlined since there is only one controlling device handling all the functionality. This added efficiency and quick response of the unit make it the most functional connection for inverters. Suppose your load demand is too great for your solar panels to handle. In that case, the charge controller works in the opposite direction and power is drawn from the batteries to make up the difference between the power that you generate and the power demanded by your load. This is expanded into the night when your solar panels are not generating any power, and your batteries are relied on to supply power to your loads. The change between operations is seamless and uninterrupted, so you will not even be aware of the change from solar to battery supply.

When it comes to charge controllers, many people don't understand their purpose. If batteries charge at 12 VDC, and you have a 12 VDC solar panel, why can't you just connect the one directly onto the other? The main reason for this is that batteries are sensitive to either voltage or current. Some batteries require a stable voltage level that doesn't spike too high, which could damage the battery's insulation, such as with gel-type batteries. On the other hand, some batteries cannot be charged quickly from a large current flowing through them, such as with AGM batteries. To avoid these two problems, charge controllers monitor and limit the amount of current that flows to the batteries as well as the voltage exposed to the batteries in order to charge them according to their manufacturer specifications. In this way, your batteries will experience a longer lifespan and will be suitably protected while charging and discharging.

These devices are typically connected to solar panel strings in the DC circuit. The advantage of having a charge controller on the DC circuit is that there are fewer losses than on the AC side, such as battery charger units consisting of a bidirectional rectifier and filter unit. Battery chargers that are connected to the AC circuit are more commonly seen in grid-tied solar systems, as they will charge batteries from the solar power and the grid without discerning between the two. There is no grid with off-grid solar systems; therefore, batteries will only be charged from the solar panels. Additionally, these batteries act as the source of power when the solar panels are not generating power, so if they run out of charge, there is no power at all. This differs from grid-tied systems where the grid can still charge the batteries even if the solar panels cannot.

Solar inverters that have a built-in battery charger system are preferable to using two different devices. A lot of this has to do with the intelligence that is built into modern-day inverters. Most leading brands have what is known as a human-machine interface (HMI) touch screen and a connection to the internet. These devices often have a read-only or adjustable phone application that you can use to connect to your inverter from your phone. The displays are very useful and include total power generated by your solar panels, percentage of charge on your batteries, your load demand at any given time, and trending data for you to track your average power usage and plan better. You will also see if it makes sense to expand your solar array or battery bank based on your needs in this way.

These features are typically available for you no matter where you are, provided you have an internet connection and provided your inverter has the capability and internet connection. It is password-protected, so there is very low risk when it comes to cybersecurity. Most modern systems are equipped with a view-only mode, which allows you to see all of the settings and live data but not change anything. This secures you from someone logging into your system and reducing the efficiency or changing settings that don't work best for you. We live in the age of information, and the more data you are able to gather and observe, the easier it is to monitor, repair, or carry out maintenance on your system. If you note that the power generated by your solar panels is lower this month than the previous one, then perhaps you should clean your panels and see what impact this will have. It's also a key indicator as to how well your batteries are aging. Inverters equipped with battery charge controllers will also have basic monitoring functionality to inform you if there is a problem with your batteries. This allows you to replace or repair a battery before it fails or reaches its end of life, leaving you in a blackout situation.

Specifying Your Fuses

Another feature included in your inverter that you should look out for is having built-in fuses and surge arrestors. These devices can be installed separately and are just as effective, but it saves cost to already have these devices sized and installed internally in your inverter. Also, make sure the inverter is lightweight and easy to install. Most inverters will come with a wall mount kit that allows you to drill and mount the inverter into a wall easily. Make sure that you select the right mounting kit based on the wall type. Metal, wood, and concrete will all have slightly different mounting kits based on materials best suited to keep the inverter sturdy.

If your selected inverter is not equipped with built-in fuses, then you will have to specify and purchase them yourself. It's important to identify the areas where fuses will be most practical. If you have a distribution board on the AC side of your inverter, then all protection devices should be mounted in there. This means that you need to worry about fuses coming into your inverter from your solar panels. These fuses need to be mounted somewhere, and typically what people will do when installing fuses is to use a combiner box. A combiner box links all your strings of panels together and has fuses and surge arrestors built into it. Your solar panel string lengths and panel sizes need to be considered when specifying your fuses. The more panels you have in series, the more current will be drawn from the solar array. This is also relevant because the rated total load current of solar panels, typically at 25 degrees Celsius, or 77 degrees Fahrenheit, is less than 10% different from the solar panel fault current. Essentially, the fuse sizes have to be very precise in order to avoid blowing a fuse when the solar array is operating correctly and not having a fuse blow when there is a legitimate short circuit fault. Additionally, not all fuses are suitable to use in DC circuits, so you need to specify that the fuses will be used in a DC system and what the expected voltage will be. Fuses are typically rated for 1,000 VAC, but this would only be suitable for use in DC systems of just over 700 VDC. This is why caution is needed when choosing your solar system fuses. Suppose you have a single string of panels. In that case, you only need to refer to the maximum operating current and fault current of a single panel in order to specify your fuses for a string connected in series. If the full rated current is 9 A and the fault current is rated at 11 A, then you should ideally choose a 10 A fuse in order to protect your string from short circuits (Clifton, 2016).

Chapter 6:
Build Your Own Solar Power System

The process of taking the theory covered in the above chapters and putting it into a physical installation requires some fundamentals that are necessary to consider. This chapter will look at practical ways to purchase the right equipment, install it correctly, and prove the system works the way you designed it. As with all designs, it is always good to test the system in a simulation before you buy so you don't find that it isn't correct or as effective as you had anticipated after going out and spending the money. There are many online resources that are free of charge, and we recommend Helioscope. It is a paid software, but there is a 30 day free trial that you can make use of. In the software, you can mimic how your solar panels will be installed, specify the exact inverter and battery backup, and the software will determine how much energy you will be able to capture over the year and pick up if there is something that you have specified which simply won't work. It's safe to say that the energy output from solar panels varies from summer to winter. Surprisingly, solar panels often perform better in the winter months because many places are drier and do not experience as much rainfall or snowfall during the winter. This increases the amount of daylight sun hours per day, increasing the quantity of energy generated by the solar panels. Another point is that solar panels have a higher efficiency when kept in cooler conditions with high levels of sunlight. They typically perform best at around 20 degrees Celsius or 68 degrees Fahrenheit, but it can vary. Temperatures above 25 degrees Celsius or 77 degrees Fahrenheit result in a degradation of energy efficiency (Almerini, 2021). Because of this phenomenon, winter months often lead to more efficient solar power generation.

20° C or 68° F

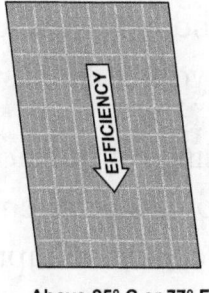
Above 25° C or 77° F

However, due to the reduced number of hours of sun in the sky during the day, you will likely see a drop in daylight sun hours and energy produced throughout the day. Moreover, most users have higher energy requirements in the winter months than they do in the summer months due to additional lighting and, potentially, heating devices that are used in winter. It's important to know your winter and summer power demands so that you don't size your system for one season but neglect the other. This may not be relevant to you if you are installing a solar system on a holiday home or RV, which you only make use of in the summer, but it is still an important consideration when sizing your solar system. Software such as Helioscope is user-friendly and takes you through a step-by-step guide to size your system according to the theory you have learned and highlights areas you may have missed along the way. It will automatically consider your geographical location, predict meteorological data based on historical data, and help you see what you can expect to get out of your solar system.

Building on this note, one of the first things you need to decide when installing your solar panels is to angle them to capture the most energy from the sun. The angle of the sun shifts between winter and summer. If you live in the northern hemisphere, the sun will not rise due east and set due west. Instead, it rises and sets further south, and how far south is dependent on the seasons. The sun will rise and set further south during the winter compared to the summer, which can have a massive impact on how much power you can generate. The thing to consider here is how much you should tilt your solar panels towards the south in order to capture the most sunlight possible. Of course, this is reversed in the southern hemisphere, where the sun rises and sets to the north.

It's a good idea to measure the space where you want to install your panels before you go out and purchase them. Measuring the space also involves verifying the areas that will receive sunlight throughout the day and which areas may experience shade. Consider this with the different times of the year, as a shadow may not be cast during the summer months on a certain area, but is cast in the same area during winter. It's also a good idea to decide where you wish to install your inverter, battery charger, and batteries. This will help you determine the cable route that you will take when installing your DC cables from your solar panels to your inverter. Also, consider where your existing AC DB is located if this is relevant to your installation.

If you are installing your panels on the roof of a house, what type of roofing is it? Corrugated iron and tiles require different mounting clips to secure the panels to a rigid structure, such as the roof.

Also, consider that you will need to clean your solar panels at least once every few months. Installations aren't just about what is convenient for you, but also what is practical in the future, especially regarding maintenance and replacement work that you may have to carry out in the future.

Now is a good time to consider the tools that you will require for installing the solar system. For the most part, the tools are relatively simple. A multimeter of some kind is highly recommended so that you can measure each solar panel as well as voltage, earthing, and frequency in your AC circuit. It's a handy tool while installing and testing your system to prove that it is working how you designed it. You will need standard handheld tools such as screwdrivers, especially a small, flat screwdriver that is commonly called a terminal screwdriver. This tool is typically used for terminating wires in electrical installations. A socket set, spanners and Allen wrenches are useful to have, as many inverters and mounting structures will require that you have these tools.

You will also require wire cutters or side cutters in order to cut cables or wires where needed. If you are using a larger cable with armoring, you may require a knife such as a Stanley knife to cut through the cable's outer sheath before stripping the armoring. It is useful to have a long nose and standard pliers for this purpose as well. Wire strippers are useful to strip the insulation off the ends of wires off to mount a connector clip, lug, or bootlace in order to connect the wire to a terminal of some kind. If you do not have wire strippers, it is possible to strip wires with side cutters or wire cutters.

The next tool is essential for electrical installations, and that is a crimping tool. This tool is used to crimp the wire with a lug, bootlace, or connector clip. In almost all electrical installations, these terminations are used instead of using bare copper or aluminum.

Crimping MC4 Connectors

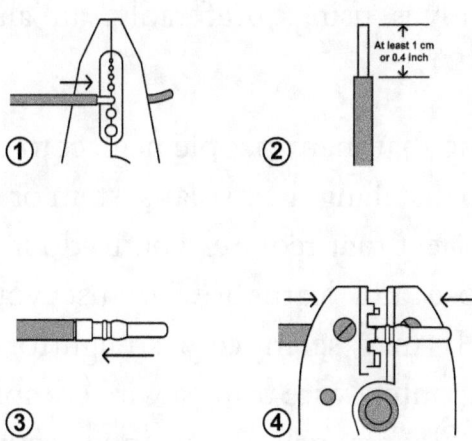

There may be an additional need to have some power tools handy. It is ideal to use battery-powered tools, as they are more practical with installations such as solar systems. A battery-powered drill and angle grinder should be suitable to cater to all of your power tool needs.

The method for installing your solar panels is quite straightforward once you can identify the surface you are installing. A rooftop mounted solar system will vary from a ground-mounted system or a flush-mounted system on an RV or boat. Some cabins do not have a tilt angle that benefits from angling it towards the sun. In order to mount the panels so that they can capture as much power from sun up to sundown, it may be more practical to build a mounting structure to maximize the panels' alignment with the sun, which involves using, preferably, an aluminum frame.

Something that many people neglect to do when it comes to installing their solar system or carrying out any project that requires you to do it yourself is to choose and learn how to use your tools correctly. It may seem very straightforward to crimp a lug onto a wire using a wire crimping tool, but many people will do it incorrectly. Even electricians often fail to follow best practices when making use of handheld tools. This results in poor workmanship and faults that would have been easily avoided if the installers had used their tools correctly. The more you use your tools, the more using them becomes second nature to you, but the first few times you use a new tool may feel unusual.

This goes for all the simple tools that are required for this installation. When stripping the insulation material off of wires using wire strippers or side cutters, be sure to strip off the right amount for the lug, clip, or bootlace that you intend to fasten onto the wire. Lugs require a short section of approximately 1 cm, or 0.4 inches, of the conductor (typically copper) to be exposed on your wire. Next up is to put the lug over the wire with the clamp section over the live conductor and the insulated section over the wire's insulation. You also need to make sure that you crimp the lug on the right way around. When a lug is crimped, there should be no copper or live conductor strands sticking out on the live connection part of the lug. The insulated part of the lug should also have a snug fit over the wire conductor without any live parts of the wire being exposed here. You can test how well a wire is crimped by pulling on it to confirm that it won't slip off the wire at any point.

This is just an example of how to use one of the handheld tools that many people aren't familiar with. There are many resources, including YouTube or even the supplier of the tools, that you can go to in order to learn good tool work practices. This preparation and learning activity may seem trivial, but it is a useful skill to have for any DIY project moving forward.

All new installations that you make to your home or vehicle are based on international or local standards. There are wiring standards, sizing standards, and aspects that will directly affect your solar installation. There is a good chance that these standards will not directly impact you in going off-grid, but there is a reason that they have been drafted, and you should not ignore them. It encompasses every small detail that you can possibly consider in your system, from the inverter you select, to earthing and safety requirements, to the mechanical reliability of your structures. Building a solar system that adheres to international standards means that you will automatically install a legal, ethical system and fits your requirements as need be.

RV Mounted Solar System

When it comes to RV solar systems, you want to mount your panels straight to the RV roof to reduce any drag you might experience while driving. It is possible to mount a rooftop system that is adjustable once you are parked to absorb more sunlight, but this may not be the best option. It has a higher initial capital cost and means that you have moving components that may require replacing. It also means that you have to get up onto the roof to adjust the angle every time you stop, which isn't a practical option. It also means that you need to ensure that the solar panels are flush and secure when you wish to drive again.

A simpler solution is going with a rooftop mount system that is flexible and does not adjust. You also don't want to drill too many holes in the roof to reduce the risk of leaking. There are great sealants available on the market that prevent leaking, but they are less effective than a system that does not require drilling to mount solar panels. There is the option of using double-sided tape that is highly resilient to environmental conditions and will adequately secure your solar panels to the roof. One such type of double-sided tape is very high bond (VHB) tape. It varies in length and width, but a good option from a reliable manufacturer to use when mounting your panels to the roof would be 3M 4941 VHB tape (Dennis, 2019). This tape is very durable and is very good at maintaining its adhesive properties even with large temperature fluctuations. When applying this tape, the surface that you mount it to must be clean. Making use of alcohol or methylated spirits even after washing the surface clean is a good idea. This will reduce the risk of dust or particles getting caught in the area that you will stick the solar panels to. The disadvantage of using this type of tape over using a drill and mount system is that you will have difficulty removing the panel at a later stage if you wish to remove or replace it.

If this is a concern that you have, then opt for drilling and tapping with a flush mount kit for the solar panels of your choice. You will have to add sealant around each area you have drilled and test that the sealant works effectively. Self-leveling sealant is readily available and will be required for the DC wires to be installed from the solar panels outside the RV to the inverter, batteries, and charge controller system on the inside.

Boat Mounted Solar System

A boat-mounted system has a lot of similarities to RV-mounted systems. The main thing to consider with a boat-mounted system is that there is a lot of moisture. The panels and outside will almost certainly get wet with saltwater rather than just rainwater (depending on whether you have a freshwater or saltwater application in mind). Corrosion at sea level is notoriously bad, and this factor shouldn't be ignored with your solar system either. Fortunately, solar panels and solar wire connectors (typically MC4 connectors) are rated to handle this type of environment. It is still good practice to clean your solar panels with fresh water frequently, just as you would the rest of the deck on any boat. Soap water and clean freshwater are all that you need.

It's also of note to point out that, in a boat installation, there is a lot of movement on deck, and the movement of a boat results in a lot more impact style motion compared to driving on the road in an RV installation. This could result in areas that have been sealed being weakened or cracked over time, which could lead to a leak from the exterior to the interior of the hull. In order to prevent this from occurring, you should use high-quality sealant that is rated for marine applications.

These are readily available from hardware stores, and this is an area where you shouldn't worry about cost-saving and should focus on purchasing a high-quality product. It's also advisable that you buy excess sealant to have on hand in the future in case you have any issues with leaking due to natural wear and tear.

SMALL HOME OR CABIN MOUNTED SOLAR SYSTEM

This type of installation is almost always going to be made up of rigid solar panels. The system is non-mobile; therefore, the weight and air resistance would not be as much of a factor as with RV's, boats, and other mobile solar systems. A word of caution here is to confirm that you will not compromise the integrity of the existing structure where you mount the panels. Whether big or small, all cabins and houses are designed to carry a certain weight on them. This usually takes into consideration various roofing tiles and extreme weather conditions that exert additional force on them. They also cater to water or snow build-up, and even the weight of a person walking over them. Now, add the weight of a dozen or so solar panels, each weighing around 20 kilograms, or 44 pounds, then add frames, wires, lightning rods, and all additional support brackets that may be required. This could add as much as 300 kilograms, or 660 pounds, of additional weight on top of your roof, which is a large additional weight. The last thing that you want is to have your roof collapse when you go up to clean your panels or have the panels act as a sail in the event of high wind, ripping them off of your roof.

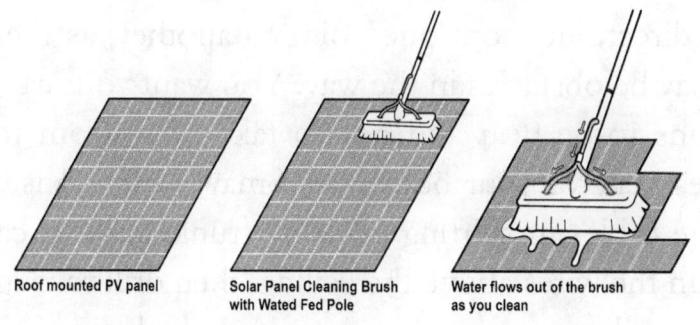

Washing Roof Mounted PV Panels

Roof mounted PV panel | Solar Panel Cleaning Brush with Wated Fed Pole | Water flows out of the brush as you clean

It's also important to consider your access to running water, particularly with enough pressure to clean solar panels mounted on top of the roof of a structure. Running water is ideal to use in order to clean your panels. You also need to consider having a ladder to easily gain access to the panels in order to clean them. Additionally, mounting the panels on top of roof tiling or corrugated iron requires mounting, which may compromise the waterproofing of your roof. Be sure to test that you have adequately sealed the roof after you have mounted the panels before experiencing rainfall. Take care when determining your cable route when taking the DC wires from the solar panel strings to the location in your home where you have decided to mount the solar inverter, preferably close to the DB. The shorter your cable length is, the fewer losses you will experience, and the less cable you will have to purchase. This doesn't mean that you should run a direct line from one point to another, as there may be obstacles in the way. You want your cable runs to be neat and not to take away from the aesthetic of your home. You may want to install the cables in skirting or cable trunking. You can run the wires above the ceiling, then drill through the ceiling and run the wires down to the inverter. In this way, you will only have to worry about sealing this point in the roof down to the inverter. It will also avoid having the eyesore of wires running through your living space.

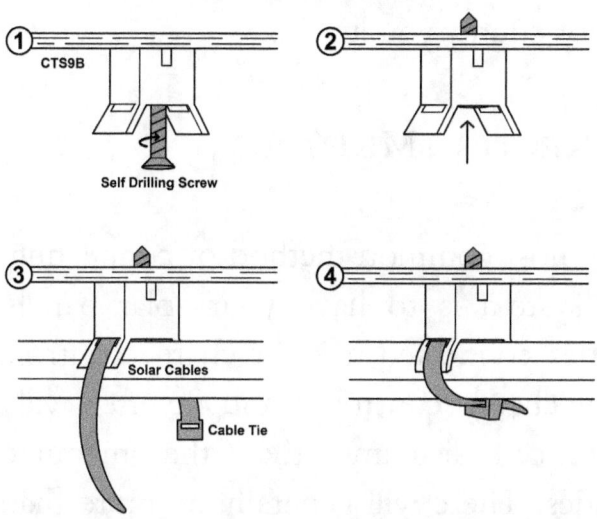
Cable Management Using Cable Ties

Don't forget to keep vermin out of the areas where electrical wires will be located. Rats and other rodents are nasty with this, as they will eat their way through the insulation of your wiring and cause a short circuit and loss of ability to generate power. Make use of flame retardant foam where necessary to keep vermin out and remove the fire hazard that comes with using regular sealant spray foam.

Solar systems on any home can drive up the property value substantially. However, this does also come with additional expenses when it comes to home insurance policies. These premiums will inevitably go up due to the addition of a solar system on the roof. It may also impact your property tax rates, depending on the country, state, or county you live in.

CONNECTION METHODS

The most common method of connecting your solar system is to have your solar panels and batteries connected to your charge controller. A typical charge controller and inverter will have connection diagrams that the manufacturer provides. There will generally be more than one option, but there will always be a recommended setup that matches your requirement.

The most common connection between the primary components is having a common negative terminal between the battery charger, solar panels, and batteries. In DC circuits, you always want to have the same reference voltage. In many installations, this negative terminal of a DC circuit is earthed, such as in cars. However, in solar systems, it is highly recommended that the negatives are not earthed. There are circumstances where this is required, but a good rule of thumb is to leave the negative terminal floating unless the manufacturer explicitly recommends that you earth them. The term "floating" is used to describe a point that may be earthed but is intentionally left without an earth reference point.

The inverter will have a positive and negative input from the batteries as well as a bypass connection from the charge controller, typically on the positive input. The charge controller controls this bypass connection. When the batteries are fully charged, excess power is bypassed from the batteries and connected directly to the inverter.

The inverter will then have a connection on the AC side to your load via a DB. This connection is via an AC cable. There is typically an isolation and protection device in the DB that acts as an incomer. The solar panel power is an incoming power to be distributed to where you require it.

Some inverters directly input from the batteries with a built-in charge controller and a direct connection to the solar panels. These units typically have no maximum power point tracker (MPPT) connections or a built-in MPPT connection. Other solar inverters have input from solar panels via an external MPPT. An MPPT is essentially a converter device that optimizes the balance between the DC voltage of the solar panels, your battery bank, and your AC system. It is beneficial to have more than one MPPT device built into your solar inverter or housed externally. Two separate units can monitor and optimize the power generated by solar panels oriented in different ways without incurring losses across your whole solar array.

When you hook your battery system up, you need to refer to the voltage rating of the charge controller and solar inverter battery input. Many of the products available on the market are limited to 12 V or 24 V, so connecting your batteries in a 48 V configuration is not a viable option. Suppose you were to connect a series of batteries resulting in a 48 V configuration to an MPPT or inverter input that is only rated for 24 V. In that case, you will damage the insulation and other electronics inside the device. Fortunately, most devices have built-in over-voltage protection, which will blow in a similar way to a fuse if the voltage level exceeds the rated voltage. These components, known as metal oxide varistors (MOVs), will have to be replaced if they are damaged in this way, and your device will not be able to operate until this is done.

You have two options when connecting multiple batteries: Connect them in either a series or parallel configuration. If you connect them in series, their voltage will increase, whereas when you connect them in parallel, their voltage will remain the same. The power goes up with the same proportions in both cases. In the case of a parallel connection, the current, or amps, supplied doubles instead of the voltage. It is always recommended that you use an even number of batteries and match your connections throughout. If you want to make up a 24 V battery setup, it isn't good practice to use three 12 V batteries. Suppose you were to put two batteries in parallel and connect these two in series with one more battery. In that case, you will be able to achieve your overall 24 V system. Still, the battery alone will have a lot more current flowing through it, which typically leads to heating issues, charging problems, and a reduction in the battery lifespan.

Ensure that the wires you use to connect your batteries are thick enough to handle the current that will flow through them. It is common practice to clamp lugs onto these fairly thick wires and add heat shrink wrap to maintain the insulation and avoid flashovers of any kind. Heat shrink is an insulating material, similar to insulation tape, but it does not use glue or other adhesives that wear over time. The heat shrink wrap is placed over the point where the lug and wire connect, and when heat is applied, the insulation material shrinks to fit snugly over the connection point.

Using Heat Shrinkable Tubes

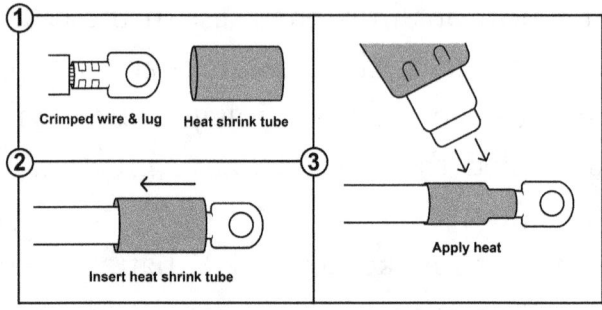

It's also good practice to install a fuse, or DC-rated circuit breaker between your DC devices. This implies that you require a DC circuit breaker or DC-rated fuse in your connections between your battery charge controller and batteries and between your batteries and your inverter battery inputs. The added benefit of having these devices is that they can act as safety isolation devices if you need to do any maintenance or replacement work on your DC system. When working on your batteries, you should turn the circuit breaker off or open the circuit using the circuit breakers between the batteries and charge controller and between the batteries and inverter before you work on them. This will reduce any risk of electrocution or injury from the batteries discharging through you when working on them.

This can be expanded into protection or isolation devices on the output of your inverter. All DBs that feed your loads should have their own protection devices, such as fuses or circuit breakers. Circuit breakers are the preferred method in these installations as they can be reset and used for up to 10,000 operations. In comparison, a fuse will operate once and burn out, requiring replacement. Fuses respond quicker than any other protection device, but a circuit breaker is preferable in the case of small household loads, even though it takes between three and five times as long to trip. Fuses will blow within 20 milliseconds of a major short circuit, whereas circuit breakers will typically trip after around 100 milliseconds. This doesn't add a significant amount of risk for small power systems, such as homes, RV's, and other small-scale solar systems.

Chapter 7:
Blueprints And Equations

In order to fully understand and implement the theory introduced above, you will need some common equations to calculate your requirements. The last thing you want is to undersize your solar system and be left in blackout scenarios on a frequent basis. It's also detrimental to oversize your solar system and end up paying excessive amounts for a system that you don't fully utilize. If your system can handle a house, but you only require it for your RV on weekend getaways, then you may have oversized your system. This is commonly referred to as an overdesign. There is nothing inherently wrong with overdesigning your solar system, only that you will end up paying more for the system than required without reaching a return on investment for the system.

When calculating the size of your solar system, you need to look at the loads that you will supply with it. Now is the time to look at the power or current requirements of the combined loads and determine how often the loads will be connected and how much power they will draw at any given time. If you are supplying three sockets rated for 15 amps, it doesn't mean that you will be using 15 amps 24 hours per day. The two factors that you need to look at are the frequency of using loads and how much of the loads will be used at any given time. With a 15 A socket outlet, you may be using 10 A, so you would be oversizing your solar system to cater for this. In the same way, you could size your backup battery storage to supply these loads for 24 hours of the day only to realize later that a lot of loads will be for things that only draw power for half of the time.

Let's start by looking at how many batteries you require for your needs. We will also consider how many solar panels you require and the type of inverter you require. The best inverters on the market have a battery charger module installed in them, as discussed in Chapter 5. These units typically have more than one MPPT to connect strings of panels angled in different ways to maximize the peak sun hours of different seasons. That being said, you need to know what is required from an inverter as well as its efficiency. Furthermore, there are things that manufacturers and distributors typically wouldn't disclose to an end-user that will be discussed in this chapter. An end-user is the description that manufacturers use to describe a person or company that will use their products. This separates them from distributors or stockholders who sell the products on behalf of the manufacturer. The ratings that manufacturers display on their datasheets are legitimate but are often based on ideal circumstances. In reality, some losses are taken that decrease the efficiency of products, but most manufacturers do not elaborate on this in detail, as it shows the limitations of their product. This is not openly displayed by competitors either.

A typical small home with two bedrooms and two bathrooms will require about eight sockets. Assuming each socket is rated at 5 amperes, there will be a total available capacity of 40 amps. That being said, it is not as though you will require a full 40 amps at 110 VAC throughout the day. Some loads will only be needed through the night, such as lights. Some loads will only be needed when you engage the load, such as swimming pool pumps. You need to consider your coincidence factor. This relates to how often loads are on. It's perfectly fine to consider your microwave when sizing your solar system, but, realistically, how often is your microwave running? This is a simplified definition of the load factor of a system. This is also why the main incoming circuit breaker from the utility is sized smaller than the addition of all the feeder breakers to household loads. You do not have everything running simultaneously and do not use the amount of electricity that you may believe that you do at any given point in time.

This coincidence factor is defined by how often you have your loads running on an average basis, and you should always cater to a worst-case scenario when you run loads more often than usual. It is basically figuring out how often your loads will run together because loads running together will draw a large amount of power. If you have a 15 A socket and three loads that require 5 A each, how often will you run these three loads together? It's like running your fridge, toaster, and microwave at the same time. This would be a highly unusual scenario, so perhaps you would only ever run two out of these three loads at any given time. What these two fundamentals translate to is that you may have a 15 A socket but will probably only ever have a maximum of 10 A being used 10% of the time, and it may only run 5 A the other 90% of the time. This can help you in specifying your battery storage requirements. In order to calculate your battery size from your current or power requirement, you need to make use of the following equations:

Power (W) = Current (A) x Voltage (V)

Energy (Wh) = Power (W) x Time (Hours)

Battery demand (Ah) = Energy (Wh) / Battery voltage (V)

Battery size (Ah) = Battery Demand (Ah) / Depth of Discharge (%)

Number of batteries = Battery size (Ah) / Single Battery size available (Ah)

Basically, if you wish to power a socket rated for 15 A at a 10 A level for a 12 hour period, then the battery size you require can be calculated in the following way:

Power = current (10 A) x voltage (110 V, the standard voltage in the US)

Power = 10 x 110 = 1,150 W

Energy = 1,150 W x 12 hours = 13,800 Wh

Battery demand (Ah) = Energy (Wh) / AC Voltage (VAC) = 13,800 Wh / 12 V = 1,150 Ah

Now, let's assume that the battery that you wish to select has a depth of discharge of 60%:

Battery size (Ah) = Battery total rating (Ah) / Depth of discharge (%) = 1,150 Ah / 0.6 = 1,917 Ah

Next, you need to take into consideration a battery rating that you may have selected. The battery datasheet will provide you with the Ah rating as well as the depth of discharge. Assume you wish to use 200 Ah batteries and that the 60% depth of discharge used above is in line with the batteries' capability:

Number of batteries = Battery requirement (Ah) / Battery rating (Ah) = 1,1917 Ah / 200 Ah = 9.5 (round up to 10 batteries)

This doesn't consider your coincidence and load factors, which will decrease the number of batteries that you require considerably. Let's say that you wish to have power available for your 15 A socket but will only use a 5 A load for a total of 24 hours to power a fridge. Let's say that you have an additional two 2 A loads that you will only use half of the time. Let's assume one of these is to feed your lights, and the other is to power electronics to charge your phone and other devices. This means that your coincidence factor is 1 for the 5 A fridge load and 0.5 for the 2 A light and charger loads. Now, to determine your coincidence factor, you must consider how often the loads will run simultaneously. As we have mentioned, the fridge will run the entire time, coinciding with both the other loads. However, how often will you run the lights and charging devices together? Most likely, only at night when you require the lights, so you can assume a coincidence factor of 0.75. This means that three-quarters of the time that these devices operate, they will be operating simultaneously. Your overall load demand changes substantially because of this and can be worked out as a percentage of the original 10 A that you had planned for using the following simplified weighted equations:

Load Demand (A) x Load factor (%) x Coincidence Factor (%) = Actual Demand (A)

This can be used to calculate each contributing load and added together to come to a weighted average. In this example, we have three loads to consider as follows:

1. Fridge Load Demand (10 Amps) x Load Factor (1.0) x Coincidence Factor (1.0) = Actual Fridge Demand (5 Amps)

2. Light Load Demand (2 Amps) x Load Factor (0.5) x Coincidence Factor (0.75) = Actual Light Demand (0.75 Amps)

3. Charger Load Demand (2 Amps) x Load Factor (0.5) x Coincidence Factor (0.75) = Actual Charger Demand (0.75 Amps)

Total of the Actual Demand Loads = 5 Amps + 0.75 Amps + 0.75 Amps = 6.5 Amps

This is essentially 65% of the size you had catered for, meaning that the 10 batteries you initially thought you would require could be reduced to eight units, as an even number of batteries is ideal.

This is just a simple rule of thumb method to calculate the basics without considering all the complex factors that can go with it. This rule of thumb calculates how many batteries and panels are required, what your cable size should be, and what inverter rating you need is accurate by over 95%, so it's a good starting point for your system (Energy Matters, n.d.). You may go through a few more iterations of your design after the first one. This is particularly true if the original cost is very high or if the inverters, batteries, and panels on the market don't accurately match your design. You may also find that you hadn't considered a factor, such as the DC voltage of your strings, and that changes your entire design.

One of the most important aspects to consider with your solar system is weight. This is especially true for a system mounted on the roof of a house or a structure, such as an RV. Most vehicles will be constructed with a chassis or body that can support additional weight but may completely alter gravity. With any moving body, the center of gravity completely alters the handling of a vehicle. Turning will be more sluggish, and the risk of rolling or suffering from understeer is a major concern. Understeer is when you turn the vehicle, but it feels as though it has a delay and pulls you toward the straight line of your trajectory for your approach to a turn.

For non-mobile installations, the primary concern is the structural integrity of the installation. If you have a rooftop that was constructed to hold roof tiles only, and you feel as though you cannot walk on the roof to inspect it because it is creaking under your weight, then the chances of that same roof being able to support several solar panels are next to nothing. Each individual solar panel that is 2 m by 1 m, or 3 ft by 6 ft, weighs roughly 20 kilograms, or 45 pounds, excluding the mounting structure and equipment required for it. This is not considering the additional force experienced from wind, rain, hail, snow, or any other weather condition.

You must be aware of the structure you will mount your solar panels on, where the points of reinforcement are, and how it may affect your property or vehicle insurance. Again, it is essential to highlight the kill switch and minuscule increase in fire risk of a solar system in any installation to keep a low insurance premium on your asset. When sizing your load requirements, it is best to look at your structure and determine the weight capacity of the existing structure. It isn't much of a concern for RVs or boats, as they can handle the additional weight on top of the main chassis. When it comes to cabins and tiny houses, the roofs may not be able to handle an additional 300 kgs or 700 pounds. Be cautious in these scenarios, as a roof may be able to take this additional weight as a static object, but that does not mean that it can handle this additional weight in a thunderstorm or if there is a significant amount of wind or snow. It may also result in an insurance nightmare where a roof was designed on standard applications of handling weather effects, and now you are adding another component to this. It's always a good idea to look at the building blueprints to see the size and weight capacity of the roof before installing your solar system. It's also valuable in this instance to enquire what the implications would be. It's not worth it to add your solar system only for a terrible occurrence, such as a natural disaster, to happen, and insurance companies refuse to cover the damage because of the addition of a solar system.

When sizing the required load of your system, particularly a house system, the best way to determine an accurate requirement is to look at your existing utility bill. The monthly bill that you are provided based on your energy meter readings is typically determined in kWh. With this reference, you should be able to average out your annual requirements for any home or holiday home application. If you are using an average of 10 kWh per day, you will be able to size your entire system based on this, including losses due to efficiency. All solar systems experience inefficiency, and you have to cater to unexpected weather conditions which may hinder your system's ability to generate power due to overcast weather or an unusually long period where your energy demands are far higher than usual.

To do this, take your monthly average utility bill over 12 months. Then take this value and divide it by an average of 30 days to get your daily energy usage. Let's say that this value comes to 5 units, or kWh, per day for a small home. This amounts to average daily usage. In order to determine your inverter size, number and size of solar panels, and number and size of batteries, you should use similar calculations used above. The primary difference is that all power used needs to be generated by the solar panels themselves. So, take your 5 kWh per day, cater to your efficiency losses, and allow a 25% safety factor.

A safety factor is an engineering term used in situations where you need to overcompensate because too many variables are unaccounted for and cannot be accurately calculated or predicted. The weather falls under this category, which is why your safety factor is required to be so substantial. Considering this, you need to allow for flexibility to cater for 7.5 kWh per day on average. Including efficiency from your DC system to your AC system requires you to implement the following calculation:

Solar Power requirement (DC kWh) = Power Demand (AC kWh) / Predicted overall efficiency (%)

Power Requirement = 7.5 kWh / 0.85 = 8.83 kWh per day. Average this up to 9 kWhdc per day.

This amount of power per day requires that you have solar panels that can provide this power in just the number of PSH per day. So, if you require 9 kWh in the space of 24 hours, then your solar panels need to generate at least this amount while the sun is up. Let's use the annual average for the sun being out and calculate PSH to be 7 hours per day. This necessitates that the DC system and solar system demand is as follows:

Solar DC demand (kW) = Calculated Demand (kWhdc) / Peak Sun Hours (Hours)

Solar demand (kW) = 9 / 7 = 1.28 kW

Now take this value and consider that days of overcast weather or reduced sun content result in a lack of generation ability from your solar panels. This can be averaged over the space of a year when considering the number of days of sun and the number of days of overcast weather. Let's assume a situation where the sun is only expected to shine for half of the year. This equates to a safety factor of two in order to ensure that you can generate enough power in a single sunny day to last over two days without any other form of power generation.

Solar Supply (kW) = Solar demand (kW) x (Days of sunlight per year / Total days per year)

Solar supply = 1.28kW x (182.5/365) = 2.6 kW

Now, this is starting to line up to a solar array size in a more understandable manner. It would be best to look at the solar panel sizes available on the market for your usage and allow yourself to generate enough power for your current system while allowing for future expansion. It is advisable to size your solar panels to cater to this demand with one additional panel and size your battery system and inverter for 1.5 times.

If you use 360 W solar panels, as 360 W and 320 W solar panels are most readily available, then you will require:

Number of panels = Power demand (kW) / Solar panel size (kW)

Number of panels = 2.6 / 0.4 = 6.5 panels

For this requirement, seven solar panels sized at 400 W or eight panels rated at 360 W should be enough for this system. Determining the number of panels that you require is the first step to take.

The next thing that you should determine is how you will hook up your solar panels. Let's take the typical example covered above, where a 360W solar panel is selected. Will you connect these eight panels in series to form a single string, which is possible to do? To calculate if this is possible, you need to find the voltage of the solar panels by referring to their datasheet. Most datasheets will list the operational voltage as Vmax or Vmp. This is the maximum operating voltage of each solar system, assuming ideal conditions of high solar irradiance and a temperature lower than 25 degrees Celsius, or 77 degrees Fahrenheit. This is not to be mistaken with Voc, which is also typically listed on solar panel datasheets. These values are when the solar panels are open-circuited or not connected to an inverter, with no current flowing through them.

When you connect solar panels in series, you add their voltage in order to get the total voltage. It is the same concept as connecting batteries together in series, with each battery adding to the overall system voltage across all the batteries. Let's use a typical voltage rating for a single 360 W CanadianSolar solar panel at 45 Volts to continue the example used above. To calculate your entire string voltage, use the following equation:

String Voltage (VDC) = Individual Panel Voltage (VDC) x Number of Panels (per unit)

String Voltage (VDC) = 45 VDC x 8 panels = 360 VDC

Now that you have the string voltage, you can specify an inverter based on the power output requirements and input voltage requirements. Most single-phase inverters rated for approximately 5 kW will handle 360 VDC as the solar array input voltage.

It's always good practice to slightly oversize your solar inverter to cater to expanding your solar array size. If you mount these eight panels now, but you realize that you require more power in five years, you want to add more panels rather than have to replace your inverter for a larger unit completely.

One of the biggest disadvantages of going with a built-in charge controller unit versus a separate unit is that, if the unit fails or you are having trouble with it, you will need to replace your entire inverter, or at the very least have the entire system offline until maintenance or repair work is carried out. Compare this to a separate charge controller, which could be disconnected and replaced at a much lower cost. Many charge controllers are manufactured to work alongside a specific solar inverter, so be sure to pay attention to which units are compatible with one another. An excellent strategy to follow is to stick to the same brand to ensure that connectivity and interconnection of control and monitoring are compatible. If you decide to use a Sunny Boy inverter, try to combine it with a Sunny Boy battery charger. Likewise, if you select a Victron solar inverter, a solar charge controller and MPPT module will work best in conjunction with this product. This is also true for warranty purposes. One manufacturer providing all the devices will make it more straightforward to identify problems, rectify them, and have replacement components sent from the manufacturer without warranty claim issues.

Conclusion

The information that you have gathered throughout this book should enable you to go out there and purchase and install your first solar system. It may have seemed daunting at first, but it is very doable when you break down the overall design into smaller, more manageable tasks. It would be best to look at what you want to get out of the solar system and determine the specific area to install the solar system. It may be on an RV, a tiny house, a boat, or even a trailer. There are so many applications for solar systems, and being able to generate your own electricity, even in remote areas, without having to burn fuel, such as with a generator, is such a valuable asset to have.

Once you have determined your specific application, you need to know some of the general terms of electricity, specifically related to solar panels. You need to have a basic understanding of your voltage, current, and power, as well as the differences between AC and DC power. Another valuable bit of knowledge is in the components themselves, including protection, earthing, inverters, and cables. There is no point in going ahead and installing your own solar system if you have no idea what the different components do and the basics of how they work. The better you understand your system, the more empowered you will be to maintain or repair the system if it stops functioning the way it is supposed to. It's also crucial to have this knowledge so that you can remain safe from harm, especially from electrocution. Suppose you want to follow quality and safety standards, especially when you install, test, or do maintenance on your solar system. In that case, you should have a solar system that meets all international standards.

When selecting your batteries, it is crucial to know the difference between the various batteries on the market. You won't want to purchase liquid lead acid batteries if an AGM battery works far better for your particular requirements. You also need to know what to look out for in batteries, including their voltage, amp hour rating, physical size, depth of discharge, and all the other pros and cons associated with each battery. When confronted with several options, you need to look at what will work best for you and offer you backup power when you need it rather than run out of energy in the middle of the night, leaving you in a blackout situation. Make sure you store your batteries in a suitable location, carry out maintenance if and when necessary, connect your batteries correctly to the charge controller, inverter, or battery charger, and don't overwork your batteries and end up reducing their life span by several years. You also need to be fully conscious of your budget and how much you are willing to spend, as well as how often you will make use of your batteries. If you spend more on a high-end battery, it will last you far longer and, possibly, save you more money in the long run.

Once you have selected a suitable battery type, you need to look at the solar panels you wish to invest in. These components, along with the inverter, will be the three most significant expenses of any solar system. Choosing the right type of solar panel for yourself is also based on your application and what you hope to get out of the system. Flexible solar panels may be more suitable for vehicles, such as RV's and boats, whereas rigid panels may be more suitable for houses. You may also want to consider monocrystalline panels if you don't have a lot of physical space but want to maximize the solar system's energy output. If this isn't as important as the cost for you, then a polycrystalline panel option may be best suited to fit your needs. Keep an eye out for panels built to international standards of safety and quality, and try to choose panels with a higher energy output to get the most power out of the fewest number of panels.

You also need to decide how you want to connect your panels. There is a limit to the number of panels that you can connect in series, and the solar inverter that you connect will also have a restriction on the number of strings and combined voltage of a string, so be sure not to exceed these limitations. It's always an option to purchase a few panels to install now and expand your system at a later stage. It's also important to note that you don't necessarily need to have a large number of panels if you have a backup battery system. If you can keep the batteries fully charged when the sun is out throughout the day, why add more panels only to waste the excess power?

Now that you have your batteries and solar panels selected, you need to look at the type and size of the inverter that you need. You may require having more than one MPPT on your inverter to capture the early morning and late afternoon sun more effectively. This is a great feature, as it allows you to connect two or more strings to separate inputs and maximizes your power generation capabilities throughout the day. It's an ideal way to do this without the expense of a tracking system, where the solar panels track the sun in the sky throughout the day. Another important consideration when selecting your inverter is confirming the efficiency, installation requirements, environmental rating (especially the operational temperature range), and power rating. You have to ensure that the inverter you select is large enough to handle the amount of power generated from your solar panels and convert that DC power to more usable AC power without significant losses.

When specifying inverters, a final note is that you should save in cost and space if you find a product that already has a built-in charge controller and connection for batteries. In this way, you will have a central unit that handles your solar panels, battery charging, and discharging and supplies AC power per your demand. Several major manufacturers produce inverters like this. Although they may be more expensive, they are worth investing in, as they are typically cheaper than purchasing both an inverter and a charge controller.

Now that you have all the major components for your solar system, you need to ensure that you have all the correct tools and equipment to mount your solar panels in your designated area safely. Do not forget that solar panels generate a voltage as soon as they are exposed to sunlight, so care must be taken when connecting the solar panels in a string and to the inverter. Electrocution from the panels themselves may not be lethal, but there are major risks, given you may be working at height and could potentially fall after being shocked.

Most tools that are required are typical electrician tools. You need a crimping tool, multimeter, screwdrivers, spanners, Allen wrenches, wire strippers, and a clamp meter for all installation and functional test work. Sometimes, if you are building a frame or mounting solar panels to an RV or boat roof, you will require some power tools, including a drill and angle grinder. It is advisable to use battery-operated power tools to have them handy in any location.

Take care to follow all manufacturer specifications when carrying out the installation. If the inverter installation guide informs you that the inverter must be installed in an upright position, then you must follow this guideline. This is especially relevant when it comes to battery storage. Great care must be taken to store batteries safely.

You now have all the basic knowledge to put together your very own solar system! As you can now see, it isn't overly complicated to follow the basic steps in specifying the major components that are best suited to your needs. You also understand the basic practices for installing your solar system safely and sticking to quality and safety standards in your installation. You now are also more knowledgeable than the average person and will be able to tell if a salesperson is pushing his product on you or is trying to find the right product for your requirements, which enables you to avoid buying unnecessary components and missing out on buying parts with significant value to you.

Building your own solar setup is very rewarding and will allow you to save on electricity costs in the long run. It will enable you to use your own power and know exactly where that power came from. Whether your system is mobile or non-mobile, you will be able to generate electricity to use from the sun, will not be impacted by problems on the grid, such as blackout scenarios, and will benefit on a monetary level in the long run. This is an investment and should be viewed as the valuable asset that it is. This is also a way for you to reduce your carbon footprint and ensure that the power you use has been generated from a renewable source. We at Small Footprint Press recognize the importance of reducing our carbon footprint to live more sustainably in the twenty-first century. Every bit counts and every individual who takes the initiative to be more conscious of their impact on the environment has the ability to make a difference. If we all make these changes in our lifestyle, we will continue to thrive and avoid damaging the environment globally. You can make a difference, and if everyone realized that their efforts and contributions made an impact, then millions more would be more proactive in reducing their carbon footprint.

You can now go out and start creating your own system. There is nothing to lose in designing and pricing your system and working out the buy-back period of the system to start you off. There is no rush, and it is better to be thorough and do things right the first time than having to make changes later, which could be time-consuming or expensive. Get your design ready, then check on the various products available to you on the market today. Look out for specials and deals to maximize your cost-saving. Once you have installed your system and have it up and running, you will wonder how you ever operated without it before!

REFERENCES

Almerini, A. (2021, March 5). *Everything you need to know about installing solar panels on boats.* Solar reviews. https://www.solarreviews.com/blog/solar-panels-for-boats

Crown Battery. (2018, April 24). *What is a deep cycle battery?* https://www.crownbattery.com/news/what-is-a-deep-cycle-battery-

Clifton, S. (2016, October 5). *How to fuse your solar system.* Renogy United States. https://www.renogy.com/blog/how-to-fuse-your-solar-system/

De Rooij, D. (2020, July 27). *Solar panel angle: How to calculate solar panel tilt angle?* Sinovoltaics - Zero risk SolarTM. https://sinovoltaics.com/learning-center/system-design/solar-panel-angle-tilt-calculation/

Dennis, R. (2019, December 20). *How to install a solar panel system on your RV roof.* RV mods - RV guides - RV tips | DoItYourselfRV. https://www.doityourselfrv.com/solar-power-4/

Energy Matters. (n.d.). *Deep cycle battery guide.* https://www.energymatters.com.au/components/batteries/#battery-explanation

Enphase. (n.d.). *What is the difference between a watt and a watt-hour?* https://enphase.com/en-us/support/what-difference-between-watt-and-watt-hour

Going Solar. (2019, March 28). *How are solar panels attached to your roof? Solar panel installation.* https://goingsolar.com/how-are-solar-panels-attached-to-your-roof-solar-panel-installation/

GridFree. (2019, August 12). *Off-grid basics - Solar power systems 102.* https://gridfree.store/blogs/how-to-articles/off-grid-basics-solar-power-systems-101

Hutchison, D., & Galiardi, S. (2019, February 21). *How solar panels work: breaking it down for beginners.* Renogy United States. https://www.renogy.com/blog/how-solar-panels-work-breaking-it-down-for-beginners/

Marsh, J. (2019, January 19). *What is solar energy?* EnergySage. https://news.energysage.com/what-is-solar-energy/

Matasci, S. (2019, January 29). *Ground mount solar panels: Top 3 things you need to know.* EnergySage. https://news.energysage.com/ground-mounted-solar-panels-top-3-things-you-need-to-know/

Proinso. (2020, May 23). *8 steps to building a DIY off-grid solar system.* https://www.proinso.net/blogs/build-diy-off-grid-solar-system/

Prowse Publications LLC. (n.d. a). *Large RV solar power blueprints*. Mobile solar power made easy. https://www.mobile-solarpower.com/the-off-grid-king-power-anything.html

Prowse Publications LLC. (n.d. b). *RV solar power blueprints*. Mobile solar power made easy. https://www.mobile-solarpower.com/the-classic-400-watt-rvs-vans-buses.html

Prowse Publications LLC. (n.d. c). *Tools*. Mobile solar power made easy. https://www.mobile-solarpower.com/tools.html

Prowse Publications LLC. (n.d. d). *Van Dweller solar power blueprints*. Mobile solar power made easy. https://www.mobile-solarpower.com/the-minimalist-great-for-small-vans-and-cars.html

ShopSolarKits.com. (n.d.). *Solar load calculator | How much solar do I need?* https://shopsolarkits.com/pages/watt-hour-calculator

Solar 4 RVs. (n.d.). *What's watt? How to calculate watt hours*. https://www.solar4rvs.com.au/buying/buyer-guides/assessing-your-solar-needs/calculating-watt-hours-wh-kwh/

Svarc, J. (2019, December 19). *Top 7 solar myths busted*. Clean energy reviews. https://www.cleanenergyreviews.info/blog/top-myths-about-solar-panels

Talens Peiró, L., Villalba Méndez, G., & Ayres, R. U. (2013). *Lithium: Sources, production, uses, and recovery outlook.* JOM, 65(8), 986–996. https://doi.org/10.1007/s11837-013-0666-4

Unbound Solar. (2020, July 8). *Grid-tied vs. off-grid solar: which is right for you?* https://unboundsolar.com/blog/grid-tied-vs-off-grid-solar

Wallender, L. (2020, July 10). *The difference between watts vs. volts.* The Spruce. https://www.thespruce.com/the-difference-between-watts-vs-volts-4767057

Weir, M. (2018, July 18). *The complete guide to solar panel mounts for boats (and where to position them)* BetterBoat. https://betterboat.com/boating/solar-panel-mounts-for-boats/

www.ingramcontent.com/pod-product-compliance
Lightning Source LLC
LaVergne TN
LVHW020930090426
835512LV00020B/3306